LEADING

— WITH YOUR —

UPPER BRAIN

LEADING
— WITH YOUR —
UPPER BRAIN

How to Create the Behaviors That Unlock Performance Excellence

Michael E. Frisina, PhD • Robert W. Frisina

ACHE Management Series

Your board, staff, or clients may also benefit from this book's insight. For information on quantity discounts, contact the Health Administration Press Marketing Manager at (312) 424-9450.

Library of Congress Cataloging-in-Publication Data

Names: Frisina, Michael E., 1955– author. | Frisina, Robert W., author.
Title: Leading with your upper brain : how to create the behaviors that unlock performance excellence / Michael E. Frisina, Robert W. Frisina.
Description: Chicago, IL : Health Administration Press, [2022] | Series: HAP/ACHE management series | Includes bibliographical references and index. | Summary: "This book applies key aspects of cutting-edge neuroscience research to illustrate how leaders' behavior affects the performance 'brain' of their team members—and overall organizational performance"— Provided by publisher.
Identifiers: LCCN 2021043440 (print) | LCCN 2021043441 (ebook) | ISBN 9781640553279 (paperback) | ISBN 9781640553248 (epub)
Subjects: LCSH: Cognitive neuroscience. | Human behavior.
Classification: LCC QP360.5 .F75 2022 (print) | LCC QP360.5 (ebook) | DDC 612.8/233—dc23
LC record available at https://lccn.loc.gov/2021043440
LC ebook record available at https://lccn.loc.gov/2021043441

The paper used in this publication meets the minimum requirements of American National Standard for Information Sciences—Permanence of Paper for Printed Library Materials, ANSI Z39.48-1984. ⊚ ™

Acquisitions editor: Jennette McClain; Manuscript editor: DeAnna Burghart; Project manager: Andrew Baumann; Layout: Integra

Found an error or a typo? We want to know! Please e-mail it to hapbooks@ache.org, mentioning the book's title and putting "Book Error" in the subject line.

For photocopying and copyright information, please contact Copyright Clearance Center at www.copyright.com or at (978) 750-8400.

Health Administration Press
A division of the Foundation of the American
    College of Healthcare Executives
300 S. Riverside Plaza, Suite 1900
Chicago, IL 60606-6698
(312) 424-2800

We dedicate this book to all the people who have contributed to making us better leaders and better human beings.

Contents

Foreword

MANY BELIEVE INTELLIGENCE and tactical prowess to be the core drivers of effective leadership, and research shows that these are important ingredients in the recipe for professional performance. A quick glance at our organizations' strategic plans and priorities, hiring processes, performance management templates, and meeting agendas will affirm that notion. An overwhelming majority of our attention is on the *whats* that we do, and not nearly enough on the *how* and *why*.

Indeed, leaders are leading—humans, processes, organizations, and more. Once we advance past the role of individual contributor, it's critical that we turn more of our energy and attention toward growing not just our technical skills but also our behavioral proficiency. Leaders with highly developed behavioral and emotional competence, who are intentionally and consistently leading from the upper brain, stand out like bright and welcoming lighthouses in our teams, our organizations, and our profession.

To lead others effectively, we must first (and always) lead ourselves effectively. The best leaders have a keen understanding of their strengths and weaknesses and actively manage both, sharing their innate aptitudes confidently and generously while humbly and transparently acknowledging deficiencies, deferring to and collaborating with others whose lights shine where their own is lacking. These leaders are aware of their positive and negative tendencies and regulate themselves effectively in order to bring their best selves to each circumstance and model an example for others.

There's an old saying: "The grass is greener where you water it." In this terrific book, my friend Dr. Michael Frisina exhorts us to bridge the knowing–doing gap, intentionally applying the behavioral practices that will better form us as leaders, building our muscle memory in those neural processes that drive leadership and executive excellence. The heavy lifting of behavioral stewardship is nonnegotiable for those who hold, or aspire to, positions of influence, because being smart, credentialed, accomplished, and well educated isn't always enough. Drink deeply of the wisdom, and experience the growth that results.

Laurie K. Baedke, FACHE, FACMPE

Preface

THE NEVERENDING QUESTION for all organizations is, how do we continue to get better at what we do? This question relates to individual, team, and organizational performance; another way of framing it is, what do we need to do to improve our performance? In healthcare, for example, the question revolves around improving patient safety, patient care quality, and patient experience. The question also affects the engagement of the interprofessional clinical healthcare team and the level of employee motivation and engagement among those who support the healthcare delivery system.

Performance is science based. Consequently, we can seek continuous performance improvement using a science-based approach to addressing two critical performance factors, as depicted in the following equation:

Performance = $f(x)$ (technical capacity) × (behavior capacity)

For decades, performance experts have sought to help organizations improve performance by focusing solely on technical capacity. This approach has not been effective in driving significant continuous performance improvement over time. Our hope is that this book will shift the emphasis away from technical capacity and toward the behavior capacity coefficient of the performance equation. Leaders can use increased behavior capacity to leverage technical capacity that ultimately will drive performance and continuous performance improvement. The simple yet profound premise of this book is that effective leadership behaviors are the key that unlocks high levels of performance excellence.

Behavior is the independent variable of the performance equation. Behavior capacity consists of the thoughts, emotions, and actions of each individual. When coupled with their level of intellect and technical expertise, this behavior capacity drives performance. Behavior is the decisions we make and the actions we take that determine performance outcomes. Rational people have complete control of their thoughts, emotions, and actions. We call this personal responsibility and accountability for performance outcomes. Since behavior is both observable and measurable, we can take a science-based approach and use behavior as the determinate factor for continuous performance improvement. Leaders ignore behavior capacity and its direct link to outcomes at their own performance peril.

In this book, we will provide a systematic, programmatic, and integrated approach to continuous performance improvement by teaching leaders and their team members how to purposefully and intentionally create the behaviors that exist in high-performing teams. We will engage you in critically examining your current behaviors, which affect the performance outcomes of your work. We will challenge you to recognize and consider alternative behavior that will contribute to your performance improvement. Finally, we will explain how to create a science-based approach to performance management in your organization—a functional methodology for managing upper brain cognitive functions, which frame effective behaviors, which manifest into high performance outcomes.

The answer to the neverending question of how we get better is for leaders to overcome bad thinking that has relegated behavior and leadership to "soft skills" that have little relevance to the science of performance. We take a scientific approach based on how the brain actually works as a performance tool. We link behavioral development directly to expected performance outcomes in the form of key performance indicators. Doing so requires a radical shift in current human resource practices, focusing on behavior development as a continuous improvement process in its own right. The development of behavior capacity, for both the leader and team members, has to be aligned with key performance indicators. The behavior changes we recommend are measurable, allowing leaders to guide their team members to the performance outcomes they desire. This is what leading from your upper brain does—it helps you get better at what you do as a leader. It helps your teams perform at high levels of performance outcomes, as well.

Introduction

The illiterate of the twenty-first century will not be those who cannot read and write, but those who cannot learn, unlearn, and relearn!

—Alvin Toffler

A NUMBER OF YEARS AGO, at an American Hospital Association Leadership Summit in San Diego, author Jim Collins, of *Good to Great*, *Built to Last*, and *Great by Choice* fame, delivered a keynote address. Collins discussed his friendship with iconic management expert Peter Drucker, and described visiting Drucker's personal library and seeing the books he had written—39 published works on management and society, and two novels—all lined up in chronological order on the library shelves. That is when Collins realized that two-thirds of Drucker's books were published after the author turned 65. Drucker believed that you should never write about a topic until you had attained mastery of it. Evidently, Drucker considered mastery of a topic a lifelong learning process.

The type of lifelong learning demonstrated by Drucker is not a trivial pursuit. In the age of the knowledge-based worker, adaptability and continuous learning define the course of your career. Current reality does not permit us to treat learning as an occasional indulgence. To become an effective leader and stay relevant, you must commit to your own lifelong learning process. Think of all the jobs and establishments that did not survive the last thirty years (Sadani 2020). Here is a short list to consider:

- Projectionist
- Photocopy center
- Cybercafes
- Video cassette parlors
- Video game centers

In another thirty years, travel agents, librarians, retail cashiers, legal secretaries, telemarketers, postal workers, social media managers, and real estate agents may similarly disappear.

Not only are occupations continually going away, but new jobs are also continually emerging. In 2018, talent management experts Tomas Chamorro-Premuzic and Josh Bersin found that half of the most in-demand skills did not exist five years before. As a result of this rapid and continual change, employers now put a premium on intellectual curiosity and the desire and ability to quickly grow and adapt one's skill set.

The leadership development world does not lack suggestions on how to create a learning culture. Here is a sample of science-based recommendations:

- Reward continuous learning.
- Nurture critical thinking.
- Make it safe for people to speak out and challenge authority.
- Give meaningful and constructive feedback.
- Lead by example.
- Hire curious people and develop them in the technical areas of their roles.

All these recommendations are behavior based as well as science based. None has anything to do with technical skill, process, strategy, talent, or intellect. Executing these recommendations successfully requires leaders who are behaviorally smart—leaders whose behaviors motivate their team members to higher levels of performance while managing constant change and continuously increasing complexity. Effective leaders are committed to lifelong learning. They are constantly reinventing themselves. They have the ability to connect and ignite the part of their brain that drives continuous growth, development, and performance.

Effective leadership requires the ability to change and innovate (Morris 2015). Consequently, we are advocating for effective leaders to engage in a lifelong learning process that transcends formal learning and encompasses a dream, a curiosity, a passionate desire, and a clear, future-oriented view of an ever-changing world. This type of learning must be purposeful, continuous, and developed over a long period of time. It requires, as Aristotle indicated, dedication to the constant formation and daily practice of good habits. It also requires what we will teach you in this book—learning to lead with your upper brain.

BECOMING SMART ABOUT BEHAVIOR AS A LEADER

You do not become an effective leader without engaging in some kind of leadership development. As CEOs, senior operational leaders, human resource and organizational professionals, you have to understand that highly effective leaders are a rare commodity. Your recruitment and retention strategy requires some leadership development methodologies. But not all leadership development models fulfill their promises of producing the next generation of emerging, effective leaders. To that end, we want you to focus on three key objectives in this book:

1. Developing a systematic, integrated, and science-based approach to performance excellence using the model constructed in this book.

2.   Identifying the cause-and-effect relationships between effective leadership, workforce engagement, and high levels of organizational performance outcomes.

3.   Discovering how performance is a function of technical skills and behavioral capacity, and how behavioral skills drive technical skills to higher levels of performance.

Performance requires more than your skill, talent, and intellect. Performance requires that you have a highly developed sense of behavior awareness and function as an effective leader. You need to be able to manage in the context of process (technical skills) and of people (behavioral skills). The behavioral skill set is a combination of a leader's ability to manage their thinking, emotions, and behavior. Inability to manage in the context of people using highly developed behavioral skills affects a leader's ability to manage and execute in the context of process. Your technical skill capability will rise no higher than your behavioral skills capacity. When you are aware of your behavior as a leader you enhance your technical skills, resulting in performance at the highest levels.

Your development as a leader, and the development of others as leaders, requires a leadership development methodology and a model that you can use to build your behavioral skill capacity. As a CEO seeking to hire a new chief operating officer, you would likely receive over a hundred resumes from people totally qualified in the job's technical skills. How would you evaluate the top candidates' behavioral skills?

Typically, people get hired because of their technical skills. Professionals rarely lose their jobs because they stop being technically smart. They lose their jobs because they consistently display disruptive behaviors that derail their careers. Becker's CEO Report E-Newsletter provides continuous examples of senior-level professionals who have lost their jobs or received disciplinary actions based on behavioral skill lapses, not technical skill lapses (Ellison 2021).

LEADERSHIP DEVELOPMENT AS A STRATEGIC OBJECTIVE

A successful leadership development program aligns company strategy with an understanding of the essential leadership behaviors needed to execute that strategy. We often confuse effective leadership with mere execution of strategy and achievement of results. In reality, effective leadership is the ability to inspire others to execute strategy at a high level of performance based on the behavior impact of the leader. No matter what else leaders do to affect the performance of their teams—communicating vision, creating strategy, providing adequate resources—the ultimate success of leaders and their teams is predicated on individual and collective leadership behavior. The foundational premise of this book is that individual leader behavior is the single most important predictor of how a team performs.

In a 2021 report on performance, Gallup found that 70 percent of a team's engagement is influenced by their manager (Ratanjee 2021). Furthermore, the traditional command-and-control management style does not work for today's workforce, which expects the manager to be more of a coach than a boss. Gallup's study of more than 550 job roles and 360 unique job competencies found that leaders who create successful, high-performing teams in thriving organizations display the following behavior skills:

- *Building relationships.* Successful leaders establish connections with others to build trust, share ideas, and accomplish work.
- *Developing people.* They help others become more effective through strengths development, clear expectations, encouragement, and coaching.
- *Driving change.* They set goals for change and lead purposeful efforts to adapt work that aligns with the stated vision.

- *Inspiring others.* They leverage positivity, vision, confidence, and recognition to influence performance and motivate workers to meet their challenges.
- *Thinking critically.* They seek information, critically evaluate the information, apply the knowledge gained, and solve problems.
- *Communicating clearly.* They listen, share information concisely and with purpose, and are open to hearing opinions.
- *Creating accountability.* They identify the consequences of actions and hold themselves and others responsible for performance.

Effective leadership development requires putting people through a set of planned scenarios that require the learners to apply effective behaviors that will drive performance excellence. For example, by learning and applying the techniques of behavior-based interviewing, you acquire the skills you need to hire the most talented people available for any job vacancy in the organization.

To create an effective leadership development program, you need three essential elements:

1. You need a mechanism for identifying your future leaders based on current performance. More importantly, you need to identify criteria for measuring future potential for performance in positions of increasing responsibility.

2. You need to determine the leadership patterns that are most appropriate for the organization, taking into account the purpose and the complexity of the organization. In most cases, you will need a combination of the four leadership behavior patterns in order to align all your strategic objectives with key results. We will discuss these patterns in great detail throughout the book.

3. You also need a comprehensive development plan for leaders at all levels of the organization, including senior leadership. Every leader in the organization needs their own personal development plan, with suggestions and specific action steps for improving their effectiveness as leaders and driving performance outcomes.

We have experienced a great deal of cynicism from senior leaders who resist investing the time and money into the leadership development program we recommend. These leaders have run the gamut of other programs and assessment tools, hoping for a silver bullet to leadership effectiveness but finding only unfulfilled promises. Each new effort and new program seems to meet with the same lack of momentum and result in the same long-term struggles to sustain leadership growth, development, and performance outcomes.

We sense that frustration and readily acknowledge it. Nonetheless, the consequences of failing to create effective leaders in your organization can be disastrous. The data show that high-performing and extremely talented people do not quit their jobs; rather, they quit their ineffective leader, manager, or boss. A study by the American Psychological Association found that 75 percent of Americans say their "boss is the most stressful part of their workday." Another Gallup study found that one in two employees have left a job "to get away from their manager at some point in their career" (Abbajay 2018).

Effective leaders are essential in every organization that wants to hire and retain exceptional talent and release that talent throughout the organization to produce high levels of performance excellence. Our primary reason for writing this book is to assist you in creating an integrated and systematic structure to develop effective leadership behaviors in your organization, which in turn will drive performance.

One part of the human brain, what we call the *upper brain*, is the catalyst for performance behavior. Effective leadership is the result of a cause-and-effect relationship between performance behaviors that reside in the upper brain (growth and performance) and blocking behaviors that reside in the *lower brain* (fear and survival). Awareness and management of the tension between these two competing operating systems provides the spark to energize, engage, and enhance performance throughout the organization.

A universal truth in the life cycle of high-performance organizations is that individual breakthroughs drive organizational breakthroughs. Reducing the variability of leadership performance is critical to successfully aligning your strategy with key performance objectives and achieving the performance results you desire as a leader. Effective leadership behavior is the means to a greater end, particularly in healthcare—safe practices, high-quality care measures, and positive patient care experiences that create high levels of service satisfaction. You can get everything else right regarding the technical skill elements of performance—recruiting and retaining top talent, having the most innovative strategy and robust financial margins—but if you lack effective leadership behavior, you will never obtain the high level of performance you are technically capable of achieving.

So, the question is not whether you should have a systematic and programmatic approach to leadership development, but whether you will have an approach that gives you a return on investment in creating effective leaders and driving organizational performance. Garland and colleagues (2021, 73) tell us that healthcare leaders need a deeper understanding of leadership development systems and practices that "hold the greatest promise for strengthening leadership and improving organizational performance." Their findings indicate a link between poor organizational performance and ineffective or weak leadership.

If you are a senior leader, you should consider adding a key objective in your strategic plan: developing effective leaders. If you can set aside any cognitive bias and cynicism you might have regarding the potential return on investment, this book will help you discover how to leverage the collective technical skill potential of your teams and drive their performance using effective leadership behavior by leading with your upper brain.

HOW THIS BOOK CAME TO BE

We did not start out knowing the importance of upper brain leadership. Like you, we have been on a journey to understand leadership all our lives, and this book is our next step in that journey. We hope you will join us on this journey to increase your effectiveness as a leader, help your team members discover their purpose, and create great work results.

Michael: My journey began in 1955 in a small town in northwest Pennsylvania. There were only 9,000 people in the town where I grew up. There are still only about 9,000 people there today. The main employers at that time were Kendall Motor Oil, the Owens Corrugated Box Company, and Zippo Manufacturing Company, makers of the iconic windproof cigarette lighter.

My path through life has included a variety of work experiences. I started in the janitor closet of my hometown critical access hospital, and moved on to on-the-job training as an operating room technician. I entered the United States Army in the enlisted ranks, earned a leadership scholarship and an officer's commission, then progressed to the C-suite of the premier United States Army medical center. After a 20-year Army career, I spent 12 years in civilian healthcare leadership and operations. I have dedicated the last 12 years to being an educator, researcher, and author on leadership behaviors that drive results to the highest levels of performance outcomes.

As a teenager, I dreamed of serving people in the delivery of patient care. I have been fortunate to fulfill that dream in a variety of military and civilian healthcare organizations all over the world.

Like Drucker, I have waited until I turned 65 to capture my reflections on this lifelong learning journey and my study and practice of effective leadership, human performance, and continuous organizational improvement. It is my privilege to share the experiences and knowledge gained from that journey in this book.

Robert: When I was ten, in May of 1992, I moved with my military family to the small town of Wahiawa on the island of Oahu. We lived near the most amazing beach and surfing destination—Hawaii's famous North Shore. My older brother would pick me up after school and we would spend our afternoons (as well as our weekends) on the beach. It was an incredible experience.

Surfing taught me lessons that I carry with me to this day. You cannot catch waves as a spectator sitting on the beach. If you are going to surf, you need to get into the water and start paddling. There is nothing easy about getting on the board and trying to catch your first wave. Surfing is a lot of work and requires a lot of effort and practice. You have to want to do it. The same principles hold true for effective leadership.

Twenty years later, in the spring of 2011, I was working as senior policy adviser for the governor of South Carolina when my United States Army Reserve unit received a deployment notice to Afghanistan. A year later, I was on a plane returning to the United States, asking myself, What do I do now? I had survived a year as a combat team leader in one of the most violent, kinetic, and hostile environments in Afghanistan, trying to win the hearts and minds of uncooperative Afghans. I was unsure about my future, other than knowing that I had absolutely no desire to return to working in politics.

My father had recently retired from his second career in healthcare administration to start a consulting firm focused on leadership development and organizational performance. When I arrived home, he asked me to join him. We joked many times in those early days that we were just "two men and a laptop." Ten years later, we have built an internationally recognized leadership consulting practice, working passionately every day to help leaders learn and apply three primary principles to benefit themselves and their team members:

1. Develop an acute sense of self-awareness and self-management.
2. Create an organizational culture of performance, growth, and development for people.
3. Engage performance as a function of technical capacity and behavioral capacity.

Individual leader behavior is the single most important predictor of your team's performance. Your behavior can be disruptive—and even toxic at times—to the performance outcomes of your team. As a leader, you mess with the brains of your people at your own performance peril. Remember, leadership is not a spectator sport. Leading effectively requires you to get in the water and do the work. And if you are going to lead effectively, you have to *want* to do it.

ORGANIZATIONAL PERFORMANCE FROM PAST TO PRESENT

Our combined professional development careers span the decades from the 1970s through today. The major influences on quality achievement, organizational leadership, and performance improvement during our careers were Drucker, W. Edwards Deming, Joseph Juran, and Peter Senge. We regret that many young emerging leaders lack exposure to Drucker's practical wisdom. He had a penchant for challenging the assumptions and motivations driving people's behavior (Drucker 2008). His wisdom could help solve many of society's problems today.

The 1970s and 1980s were a period of great transformation, particularly in healthcare organizations—motivated, in part, by a massive growth in technology and a major shift in The Joint Commission's survey process. During the 1970s, The Joint Commission survey typically involved a small number of people, and the standards focused on things that ensured the organization was *prepared* to provide quality patient care, rather than on the actual quality and safety of care that patients received. In 1986, The Joint Commission shifted focus to the quality of the care itself. The Joint Commission went back to its founding principles, following every patient long enough to determine whether treatment was successful. Then they added one more step: If the treatment was not successful, they asked why not, to prevent similar performance failure on the next patient. As The Joint Commission survey process shifted to performance improvement, patient outcomes, and data-driven decision-making, leaders of healthcare systems adapted.

Adding to this shift was Stephen R. Covey's 1989 classic, *The 7 Habits of Highly Effective People*. Whereas his contemporaries focused on process, Covey focused on people. The idea that you are efficient with things (process) and effective with people created a perspective balanced between obtaining results and caring about the people producing those results. This began the tension for leaders between process focus (technical capacity) and people focus (behavior capacity).

A year later, Peter Senge published *The Fifth Discipline,* and the "ethos of learning" became the next wave of organizational and leadership transformation. Leaders once again adapted to create learning environments devoted to growth and development at all levels of the organization. Employees attended workshops and courses both on- and off-site. Performance improvement spawned an entire new field of work as consultants lectured to standing-room-only capacity audiences.

In healthcare, not only was there a renewed emphasis on the quality of care provided and on patient outcomes, but there was also a direct link created between the delivery of high-quality healthcare and patient satisfaction. Patients, viewed as customers or consumers, provided feedback on their care, which organizations used to identify performance improvement opportunities and target improvement actions. These improvement activities were supported by the scientific method of measurement and observation. The scientific method now governs all performance improvement activities—at least from the process side.

As a capstone to all these paradigm shifts, Daniel Goleman published his bestseller *Primal Leadership* in 2002. In it, he sounded a clarion call to leaders to stop ignoring the link between emotions and business performance and make emotional resonance their first priority. Doing so, he said, would allow people to flourish in their work and produce the results their leaders desired. Emotional intelligence—becoming smart about emotions, in Goleman's model—really matters for leadership success.

We want to take Goleman's concept to the next level. We want to shift from being smart about emotions to being smart about behavior—specifically, effective leadership behavior that drives performance.

Throughout these decades of change there have been discussions about the need to move away from the traditional command-and-control leadership that dominated the latter half of the twentieth century. Uhl-Bien, Marion, and McKelvey (2007) note that the historical models of leadership, particularly bureaucratic command and control, are more suited for physical production and manufacturing than for the knowledge-based work of the twenty-first century. They propose, as we do, that elements of leadership effectiveness must include aspects of organizational learning, innovation, and adaptability, each of which focuses on the leader's behavioral skill, not technical skill.

Since the early 2000s and Goleman's influential book, a host of scholars, researchers, and consultants have urged leaders to move away from acting as an expert who tells a team what to do to get results. In the emerging model, the leader is a coach who guides a team through open-ended questions to desired outcomes. With our behavior-based approach to leadership effectiveness, we tend to avoid these either/or contrasts. A variety of contexts, situations, and crises can make leader-as-expert behavior necessary and relevant to optimize the outcome.

We recognize the tension between the traditional expert leader (telling) and coach leader (asking), but we will demonstrate that leaders can adapt themselves to a variety of behaviors depending on what is most relevant to the challenge of the day. Most importantly, advances in neuroscience allow us to account for situational and environmental variables that influence effective leadership behaviors. This results in a predictive model of behaviors that will be effective for leaders and team members, especially during times of extreme stress, frustration, and conflict. An effective leader responds with effective behavior most suited to any situation or environmental variable by leading with the upper brain.

A NEUROSCIENCE MODEL FOR EFFECTIVE LEADERSHIP BEHAVIOR

Attempts to catalog human behavior into specific patterns and match those patterns to advances in human development go at least as far back as the Chinese in 2200 BCE. In ancient Greece, Empedocles created a behavior classification system in 444 BCE, and the four-quadrant model developed by Hippocrates in 400 BCE has strongly influenced modern four-quadrant models (Hamilton 2010). With the advent of technology that permits us to see the brain functioning in real time, we can now prove or disprove many of the assumptions in these types of theories.

Landy and Conte (2014) identify certain leadership theories as highly suspect in their explanation of or correlation to effective leadership, and in particular their business applications for performance outcomes. For example, great man theories examined the lives of respected leaders for factors contributing to the person's success and greatness. While popular and appealing, such theories have no supporting scientific research. The trait theory of the early twentieth century proposed that leaders possessed certain characteristics that nonleaders did not. The trait theory has made a comeback since 2000, and has broad appeal. Researchers have studied more than forty such characteristics but still struggle to identify what each trait actually means. Without scientific research to support its claims, we should remain skeptical about adopting a trait approach for leadership effectiveness.

Constant change and increasing complexity require leaders to have a variety of complex technical and behavioral competencies. We define *competencies* as a set of behaviors, learned by practice and experience, which are necessary to achieve a desired organizational outcome, objective, or result. To be highly effective and behaviorally smart, leaders need to learn how to lead from the upper brain, which drives performance behavior and protects the lower (survival) brain from antagonism that drives survival behavior. As you will learn, the brain excels at creating performance and at sustaining survival; it just is not good at doing both at the same time.

Identifying your authentic self, behaviorally speaking, and managing that behavior consistently from one context to another is the key to your leadership success. No organization can become in performance what its leaders are not in their behavior. We believe that the most forward-thinking business leaders today should encourage and support business educators in teaching the importance of effective leadership behavior.

This book will explain how the human brain works in practical terms and help you use this knowledge as leverage to increase leadership effectiveness and drive performance outcomes. Key leader behaviors can improve or impede human performance. Our approach is science-based: By focusing on behaviors that are physical, observable, and measurable, we can improve leadership effectiveness and drive outcomes in a tangible and meaningful way.

For years, we have been teaching this approach in our keynotes, seminars, and workshops and using it in our executive coaching practice with great success. In our previous book, *Influential Leadership: Change Your Behavior, Change Your Organization, Change Healthcare*, we identified three fundamental principles (see exhibit 0.1) that create and drive leadership influence: self-awareness, collaboration, and connection (Frisina 2014). Leaders who have studied, developed, and

Exhibit 0.1 Fundamental Principles of Influential Leadership

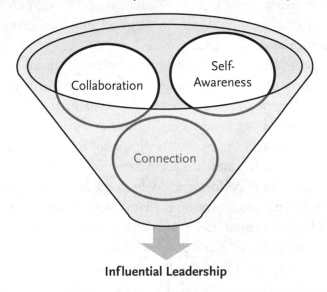

Influential Leadership

Source: Frisina (2014, 3).

applied these principles have achieved significant personal growth and attained remarkable performance achievements in their organizations.

Human performance is predicated on the ability of the human brain to function in certain ways to produce the outcomes you desire. The concepts and principles you will learn in this book and apply in your own work are the products of decades of actual practice in our own professional work and of evidence-based data from advances in neuroscience.

That is what makes this book different. Rather than applying the scientific method to process, we are going to apply it to people—specifically to leaders—and to their brains. When leaders behave in ways that allow people's brains to focus on growth, development, and achievement, then we increase the level of performance in patient safety, quality outcomes, and patient experience that healthcare leaders require and patients deserve. This scientific approach is applicable to leaders and their teams in other industries, as well. There is a clear correlation between performance behaviors and performance outcomes in any enterprise. We are providing a science-based methodology that governs performance behavior activities and is applicable to any organization.

Since our passion and purpose has always been the delivery of patient care, we will illustrate the model and principles of effective leadership using healthcare examples. Where appropriate, we will also use examples from other fields to demonstrate the universal application of our model to education, manufacturing, finance, and service organizations as well.

With the growth and development of neuroscience and real-time imaging technology, researchers have improved our understanding of the human brain and created a new vocabulary for discussing human performance. Terms such as *brain elasticity, epigenetics, dual-process theory,* and *default mode network* describe how the brain enables growth, development, and achievement on one hand, and how it enables survival through its reactions to threat, fear, loss, and anxiety on the other.

Leading with Your Upper Brain will explain why people must be able to connect and engage with their leader to connect and engage with their work. When a leader exhibits behavior that promotes psychological safety, team members' brain responses trigger their ability to focus on their work and produce results at a high level. When a leader's behavior does not promote psychological safety, team members' brains will focus on responding to fear and threat, diminishing performance. *Toxic* is the word used in the research literature to describe this kind of leadership behavior.

Wilson (2014) describes the psychological and physiological effects of ineffective leadership behavior on team members' engagement and their ability to perform at high levels. An evolutionary biologist who focuses on applying the principles of life science to business practices and organizations, Wilson believes that ineffective, toxic leadership is a plague in any social organization that lacks the mechanism to control it. In chapter 3, we will expand on this concept and how it affects our ability to drive individual and organizational performance to the highest levels.

Based on our research, effective leadership is the dependent variable that drives culture to create engagement. Engagement is the foundational behavioral skill that drives technical skills to their highest levels. Performance outcomes are the combination of three science-based behavior performance equations that create the results leaders desire and add meaning and value to people's work.

Our behavior performance model is systematic in that it links leadership behavior directly to employee engagement, which links directly to business outcomes and performance. The model is integrated in that it cascades across all leadership levels of an organization. Finally, it is backed by data, research, and performance metrics from field testing with clients to validate performance outcomes. The structure of this book reflects the behavior-based performance equations that make up our model (exhibit 0.2).

Part I, "Effective Leadership," explains the first of the three behavior performance equations. Effective leadership describes and demonstrates behaviors that focus on aligning the key objectives of the organization to the performance outcomes that leaders desire. Effective leadership also promotes the well-being and

---

Exhibit 0.2 Three Behavior-Based Equations for Performance

$$\text{Performance} = f(x) \text{ (technical skill)} \times \text{(behavior skill)}$$

$$\text{Engagement} = f(x) \text{ (culture)} \times \text{(effective leadership)}$$

$$\text{Effective leadership} = f(x) \text{ (self-awareness)} \times \text{(self-management)}$$

---

interests of the members of the organization. Leaders face a challenge: focusing on both performance objectives and the growth and development of people in the same organizational culture. The two goals need not be mutually exclusive. We will show you how effective leadership behaviors can accommodate both cultural requirements.

Part II, "Engagement," describes the second science-based equation for performance. You do not get performance without engagement, and you cannot create engagement without effective leadership and a consistent, value-based organizational culture. Engagement is people's willingness to come to work and fulfill the interests and objectives of the organization. Engagement requires an individual to choose to subordinate self-interest to organizational goals. The greater the need for individuals to preserve self-interest, actual or perceived, the more difficult it becomes for leaders to create engagement.

According to Gallup (2017), just 33 percent of American workers are engaged by their jobs. Fifty-two percent say they are "just showing up," and 17 percent describe themselves as "actively disengaged." Most employers have a lot of work to do to unlock the full potential of their workforce. Effective leadership provides the psychological safety necessary for people to focus on the needs of others. It is a function of leaders behaving in a way that allows the brains of others to focus on performance rather than individual survival, creating a natural pathway to engagement and higher levels of performance.

Part III, "Performance," deals with the capstone equation of our performance model. This section combines the elements of the previous chapters into a cohesive methodology. By using our performance model, leaders will drive higher levels of performance and simultaneously create conditions for their team members to discover meaning, value, and purpose in their work. When combined, the three equations in our model play a powerful role in overall well-being. Whenever performance does not match potential, it indicates a gap between how we are actually performing and what we could be achieving with the appropriate levels of effective leadership and personal engagement. In healthcare, when our performance does not match our potential, people suffer real harm. We are not talking about what we hope we could achieve in our level of safety, quality, and service performance. We are talking about achieving what we are already capable of doing to create a higher and consistent level of performance outcomes.

BECOMING A MORE EFFECTIVE LEADER

We believe that we are on the verge of yet another transformation in how effective leaders will lead their organizations to performance excellence. As we encourage you to adopt this model, we acknowledge a debt of gratitude to those leadership practitioners, researchers, and scholars who preceded us in this work.

We are convinced that emerging leaders will be most effective when behaving in ways that lead the brains of their team members to higher levels of performance. These leaders will learn and apply the principles of neuroscience detailed in this book and will change the way they think about themselves and their roles. They will change the way they currently communicate purpose and will create organizational cultures that focus on the growth of individuals while advancing the key objectives of the organization. Finally, these effective leaders will provide people in their organizations the ability to discover meaning and value in their work—the ability to change the world for good. You can be that kind of leader. Your journey to leadership effectiveness starts now.

KEY TAKEAWAYS

- This book fills the gap between traditional leadership theory and thinking about performance as a byproduct of technical skills, strategy, and individual talent. We offer a new way of thinking about performance that combines technical skill capacity with behavioral skill capacity, supported by neuroscience research.

- The highly effective leaders we studied for this book all have a common behavioral habit of lifelong learning. These leaders have an insatiable thirst for finding ways to continue improving in the face of constant change and increasing complexity in the world.

- When people work for an ineffective leader, their performance is always inconsistent and at levels below their potential, their capabilities, and their personal desire to achieve outcomes.

- When you have a performance system that clearly defines roles, goals, and expectations and aligns employees' work to your objectives and key results, and when you conduct regular coaching sessions with the people doing the work of the organization, you will drive performance to higher levels.

- Knowledge-based workers will resist control; they are motivated by meaning, value, and purpose in their work, not personal financial profit.

- Leadership theories of the past that lack scientific support should be approached with some skepticism.

- People who occupy leadership positions of power and authority tend to change their ineffective behaviors when they understand the effect of those behaviors on other people, how those behaviors disrupt performance, and the lost opportunities for their own continuing performance and promotion opportunities.

- Not every ineffective leader has the desire to change their behavior, regardless of the negative outcomes their behavior produces.

PUT IT TO WORK

1. As a leader, you occupy a professional position. That professional status requires you, first and foremost, to behave in a way that acknowledges your stewardship responsibility to sustain the welfare of your organization and your organizational members. Consider and respond to the following self-reflective questions:

    *   Have you ever completed a 360-evaluation tool? If so, how do you use that information to manage your behavior day-to-day?

    *   Do you give people opportunities to offer you feedback on your behavioral lapses? If yes, how is that working for you? If not, why would you not want to know how your behavior is affecting other people?

    *   You cannot change what you do not measure, and you cannot measure what you do not know. How do you measure your level of leadership effectiveness? Do you have a development plan for becoming a more effective leader? If so, does your development plan include

        –   challenges that make it difficult for you to effectively execute your job responsibilities;

        –   things you could do to improve your performance or meet your objectives more effectively; and

        –   development goals with specific behavior objectives to raise the level of your performance effectiveness?

2. Are you constantly engaged in your own lifelong learning journey?

    *   Do you have a personal set of core values? If so, what are they, and are they consistently evident in your behavior? If not, would you be willing to engage in a

values discovery exercise? (Here is an excellent resource to guide you: www.mindtools.com/pages/article/ newTED_85.htm.)

- Do you commit a certain part of your day to learning something new about effective leadership? The cumulative effects of 15–20 minutes a day working on your personal leadership development can be transformational. The following suggestions all can take less than 20 minutes a day:
  - Listen to a TED Talk.
  - Listen to a leadership podcast.
  - Read ten pages of a leadership book.
  - Read a leadership blog.
  - Read a leadership newsletter.

3. Effective leaders have a clear set of personal core values. They have formulated a personal purpose statement that keeps them mindful of their organizational duties and responsibilities. They take responsibility for ensuring that their teams, as business units, achieve expected results.

- What is the status of your organization's leadership development program?
- How do you assess your leaders' performance gaps to guide their improvement?
- Is leadership development a strategic objective of your organization?

REFERENCES

Abbajay, M. 2018. "What to Do When You Have a Bad Boss." *Harvard Business Review*. Published September 7. https://hbr.org/2018/09/what-to-do-when-you-have-a-bad-boss.

Chamorro-Premuzic, T., and J. Bersin. 2018. "4 Ways to Create a Learning Culture on Your Team." *Harvard Business Review*. Published July 12. https://hbr.org/2018/07/4-ways-to-create-a-learning-culture-on-your-team.

Covey, S. R. 1989. *The 7 Habits of Highly Effective People*. New York: Simon and Schuster.

Drucker, P. 2008. *The Essential Drucker: The Best of Sixty Years of Peter Drucker's Essential Writings on Management*. New York: Collins Business Essentials.

Ellison, A. 2021. "California Hospital COO Disciplined Over Vaccine Scandal." *Becker's Hospital Review*. Published January 27. www.beckershospitalreview.com/hospital-management-administration/california-hospital-coo-disciplined-over-vaccine-scandal.html.

Frisina, M. E. 2014. *Influential Leadership: Change Your Behavior, Change Your Organization, Change Health Care*. Chicago: Health Administration Press.

Gallup. 2017. *State of the American Workplace*. www.gallup.com/workplace/238085/state-american-workplace-report-2017.aspx.

Garland, N., A. N. Garman, P. S. O'Neil, and W. J. Canar. 2021. "The Impact of Hospital and Health System Leadership Development Practices on Bond Ratings." *Journal of Healthcare Management* 66 (1): 63–74.

Goleman, D. 2002. *Primal Leadership: Realizing the Power of Emotional Intelligence*. Boston: Harvard Business Review Press.

Hamilton, S. 2010. *Profiles Performance Indicator Technical Manual*. Waco, TX: Profiles International.

Landy, F. J., and J. M. Conte. 2014. *Work in the 21st Century: An Introduction to Industrial and Organizational Psychology*, 4th ed. Hoboken, NJ: Wiley & Sons.

Morris, L. 2015. "If You Want to Be a Good Leader, Be a Good Learner." Innovation Management (blog). Published May 26. https://innovationmanagement.se/2015/05/26/if-you-want-to-be-a-good-leader-be-a-good-learner/.

Ratanjee, V. 2021. "Why Managers Need Leadership Development Too." Gallup Workplace. Published January 15. www.gallup.com/workplace/328460/why-managers-need-leadership-development.aspx.

Sadani, D. 2020. "Learn Unlearn Relearn." LinkedIn (blog). Published December 21. www.linkedin.com/pulse/learn-unlearn-relearn-darshan-sedani/.

Senge, P. 1990. *The Fifth Discipline: The Art and Practice of The Learning Organization*. New York: Doubleday/Currency.

Uhl-Bien, M., R. Marion, and B. McKelvey. 2007. "Complexity Leadership Theory: Shifting Leadership from the Industrial Age to the Knowledge Era." *Leadership Quarterly* 18 (4): 298–318.

Wilson, D. S. 2014. "Toxic Leaders and the Social Environments That Breed Them." *Forbes* (blog). Published January 10. www.forbes.com/sites/darwinatwork/2014/01/10/toxic-leaders-and-the-social-environments-that-breed-them.

Effective Leadership

Nothing so conclusively proves a man's ability to lead others as what he does from day to day to lead himself.

—Thomas J. Watson, former president of IBM

HAVE YOU EVER had a chance to play with a Newton's cradle? The device has appeared at least twenty times in movies, including the 2015 movie *Concussion*, where it represented the National Football League's obstinate position on traumatic brain injury. It is also a popular desk toy, allegedly first sold by Harrods in London, England. We have one in our office.

Named after Isaac Newton, Newton's cradle demonstrates cause-and-effect relationships involving the conservation of momentum and the conservation of energy. It also provides a constant reminder to us and our clients about leadership behavior and its links to leadership effectiveness, leader and employee engagement, and, ultimately, performance outcomes.

Newton's cradle serves as an adequate metaphor for the performance relationships we will identify in this book. The main theme of this section of the book is the impact your behavior as a leader has on your leadership effectiveness, on team member engagement, and on performance outcomes.

Your behavior, which is a manifestation of your brain activity—thoughts, perceptions, judgments, and emotions—is a catalyst altering the nature and effectiveness of your personal and professional relationships (Leaf 2009). Imagine your effective leadership behavior as a cause and the resulting team engagement and performance outcomes as the effect. Just as one steel ball collides with the others in Newton's cradle and creates a predictable outcome, so too our behavior as leaders collides with the brains of our team members, with equally predictable results.

In part I, we will explore the cause-and-effect nature of effective leadership behaviors and the effective leadership equation, along with the two key coefficients in the equation. Chapter 1, "The Effective Leadership Equation," describes the causal connections between self-awareness, self-management, and effective leadership. Self-awareness is often cited as one of the most important characteristics necessary to develop as an effective leader; but self-management is equally important, and not something we see emphasized enough. You cannot have effective leadership without both.

Chapter 2, "Self-Awareness," explores the key elements of knowing your authentic self. Each of us has a primary behavior pattern. Lacking awareness of your behavior pattern and its effect on other people can derail your leadership effectiveness. Lack of self-awareness also has a significant impact on the organization's bottom line. Leaders who demonstrate strong self-awareness are better able to connect and engage with their team members, resulting in a higher level of performance outcomes. This improves primary business functions such as productivity and quality, directly increasing financial performance. Remember, your behavior is not a secret. Your behavior lapses are painfully obvious to everyone else. Self-awareness begins the process of effective behavior change and continuous performance improvement.

Finally, chapter 3, "Self-Management," offers you a practical strategy for adapting your primary behavior pattern to the behavior patterns of others, which creates powerful leverage for exponentially improving performance outcomes. Self-management is also the dependent variable that affects the level of your leadership effectiveness. Many people are aware of the ways their behavior adversely affects colleagues, team members, and organizational performance. The key is whether they have the desire and skills to change that disruptive behavior: Can they self-manage to produce a positive impact on the people they lead and the organization they serve?

When leaders exhibit self-awareness and self-management, their behavior is more effective, and their team members are better able to connect and ignite the growth, development, and performance part of their brains—the prefrontal cortex. We call this part of the brain the upper brain. When you connect to and ignite your upper brain, you power on your intellect, talent, and skill to create performance outcomes.

When leader behavior is ineffective, the impact on team members is disruptive and unproductive. Ineffective leadership behavior triggers the limbic system, forcing your team members to focus on managing their fear, loss, and doubt. This part of the brain—the lower brain—is built for survival. The lower brain helps us manage legitimate fear in response to external threats. Those threats, real or perceived, create three predictable human reactions: a mental reaction (confusion, loss, doubt), an emotional reaction (fear, anger, disgust), and a physical reaction (fight, flight, or freeze). When your team members spend their productive efforts surviving at work rather than thriving at work, performance suffers.

To prove this point by way of qualitative research, think about the most effective leader you have worked with in your entire career. Write a short list describing this highly effective leader using one-word attributes: "My ideal leader is . . ."

Our work with a large number of diverse teams in multiple countries produces a similar list of attributes each time we conduct this exercise. Here is a typical list:

honest	transparent	visionary	engaged
disciplined	humble	servant-like	competent
compassionate	candid	approachable	self-controlled

Is there a strong correlation between this list and the one you created?

Now, list the attributes of your worst boss: "My worst boss is . . ." In our workshop experiences, it never takes as long for people to develop this list as it does the first one. A study conducted by the American Psychological Association indicates that human beings tend to have more immediate and vivid recall of negative and traumatic life events than positive ones (Kensinger 2011). Here are the responses we consistently receive to the second question:

self-centered	selfish	arrogant	egotistical
narcissistic	unpredictable	impulsive	thoughtless
rude	callous	detached	unfriendly

If we compare the two lists, we see attributes that are almost direct opposites of one another. We also see that both lists describe behaviors. Rarely does anyone respond that their ideal leader is a financial genius or a brilliant strategist. Often, the worst boss *is* a financial genius or a brilliant strategist, but all that superb technical skill goes to waste because no one wants to work with or support this individual in producing results at a high level of performance outcomes. The truth is that the results produced by virtue of your technical skills will never surpass your ability to create highly effective, performance-driving relationships (your behavior skills capacity).

Based on the two lists you created, we will now ask you two self-reflective and provocative questions: In your current leadership role, would you say you exhibit more qualities from the first list or the second? If we were to survey your current team members and ask them about you as a leader, would they describe you with more words from the first list or the second one?

As you will soon discover, the research indisputably proves that disruptive, ineffective, negative, and toxic leadership behaviors ultimately impair the upper brains of team members. Remember, the upper brain is responsible for the executive, technical skills necessary to produce high levels of performance. Not only does toxic leadership behavior disrupt and inhibit upper brain performance, but such behavior also can lead to unwanted legal and financial repercussions, loss of engagement and burnout, mental health issues such as depression, and even thoughts of suicide. Something else to consider is that your impact on others through your actions, words, and behavior determines how people choose to remember you.

Left unchecked in an organization, ineffective leadership behavior hurts the organization and its members in significant and tangible ways. It is a matter of brain science.

KEY TAKEAWAYS

- The two key coefficients in the effective leadership equation are self-awareness and self-management.
- Human beings are wired for growth, development, and achievement. We are also wired to prioritize survival behaviors in response to threat stimuli. The human brain can perform both functions extremely well—just not at the same time.

REFERENCES

Kensinger, E. 2011. "What We Remember (and Forget) About Positive and Negative Experiences." *Psychological Science Agenda*. Published October. www.apa.org/science/about/psa/2011/10/positive-negative.

Leaf, C. 2009. *Who Switched Off My Brain?* Southlake, TX: Improv.

CHAPTER 1

The Effective Leadership Equation

Ability and capability are not about traits, personality or genes—they are about behavior. Unlike genetics or personality, behavior can be described, observed, measured and changed. As a result, both ability and capability can be increased.

—Robin Stuart-Kotze

A FEW YEARS AGO, we were presenting at the American Hospital Association's Rural Health Summit. We titled the keynote address "Becoming a Behavior Smart Leader." The conference was interactive and participants had live feeds back to their organizations to share information in real time. Their comments were also posted in an open forum for all conference participants to read. During our keynote, we asked participants to ponder the following question: Would you follow you as a leader? This question is worth your personal reflection as well.

From this meeting, a CEO posted our question on his live feed, in the open forum, and sent this response back to his organization in real time:

> I have been confronted with a very thought-provoking question during the last keynote, "Would you follow you

as a leader?" Giving this question some careful consideration, I finally I had to say "Yes—I would follow me
as a leader." The problem I have at our hospital is not
my leadership but all the pickle suckers I have working
for me.

No doubt this CEO is bright, technically talented, and has had
a successful career as a senior healthcare executive. All things being
equal, he is probably a good person in many other aspects of his
life. No doubt he has a grasp of the key technical skills required of
a chief executive and easily identified in the leadership and management literature:

- C-suite communication skills
- Change management skills
- Subject-matter expertise
- Strategic thinking skills
- Decision-making skills

The fundamental problem for this executive (and many more
like him) is the lack of behavioral awareness. Most likely, this
is the biggest obstacle he faces in becoming a highly effective
leader.

Behavior lapses are painfully obvious—except to the person committing them. Is it conceivable that this CEO has no
idea how his behavior comes across to the people whose performance is necessary to fulfill the strategic objectives of the organization? Is it possible that, having attained an executive-level
position, he has become insensitive to the fact that his individual leader behavior is the single most important predictor
of how his team performs? Could he have been that unaware
of how his response, shared in an open forum, would affect the
motivational drivers of the key members of his organization?
Can you imagine sending this response back to your entire
organization?

THE KEY TO ACHIEVING RESULTS

We all are capable of these types of behavioral lapses. Before we pass judgment too quickly on senior executives, we should mention that we have witnessed significant behavioral lapses at all levels of organizational leadership during our development engagements—and in the rank-and-file team members, as well. Yet the reality is that these lapses have the greatest impact on the organization's consistent high-level performance when they happen at the senior level. Leadership effectiveness is the primary predictor of business performance. Leadership effectiveness is the primary predictor of clinical outcomes in healthcare, too.

Often, these disruptive behavior habits wreak more havoc on daily operations when they are aimed at lower operational levels of the organization. When they happen at the senior level, the impact on key personal relationships is more evident. The higher you go in positions of authority and power, the greater the impact your behavior has on the performance outcomes of your team. Effective leadership behavior matters to the performance outcomes of organizations. It matters a lot. You may disagree with the research, you may ignore the research, but you do so at your own performance peril.

Behavior issues are important at all levels of the organization. At the top of the organization, however, your behavior skills determine the level of your performance and the overall performance of your organization. This is true for every member of the C-suite. The highest-performing teams are always led by the most effective leaders, whose behaviors are guided by their upper brains.

EFFECTIVE MANAGER VERSUS INEFFECTIVE LEADER

A particular CEO had been in the role for eight years when the board of directors retained us to assist in creating a leadership development department for the organization. Before becoming CEO, this person had risen quickly through the organization's ranks, moving from director to vice president to chief operating officer within nine years. Everyone knew the CEO to be highly intelligent, technically brilliant, hard-working to a fault, and extremely competitive. The CEO's tendency to engage in disruptive behavior affecting the overall performance of the organization was also widely known.

In our work with this CEO and the organization's leaders, we administered a behavior assessment tool designed to map people's behavior patterns into four groups (Hamilton 2010). These groups are determined by two primary measurements that compare people-oriented behavior with task-oriented behavior and faster-paced behavior with slower-paced behavior. We created a performance development plan from the assessment data, emphasizing changes in behavior to improve the overall leadership effectiveness of each leader—including the CEO.

The following is a summary of the CEO's key behaviors as indicated by the assessment tool profile and validated by personal interviews with the CEO, members of the board of directors, and the executive team:

- Decisive and direct, likes to control the work environment
- Works best with minimal supervision and maximal control
- Takes challenges easily
- Comfortable with change
- Takes action, impatient
- Self-starter
- Competitive
- Results-oriented

The behavior performance profile report included suggestions for behavior improvements that align with the six leadership performance factors. Using Hamilton's approach, effective leadership performance is typically measured along these six dimensions. When a person commits to a development plan's key goals, following the recommended suggestions for improving effectiveness produces significant improvements in performance in all six leadership factors. These behavior changes also produce significant improvements in leadership effectiveness with regard to relationships that are essential to driving performance in those core areas. Following are the key improvement suggestions for this CEO, by performance factor:

- *Productivity.* Realize that others may need time to adjust to your quick decision-making style. Having multiple projects running simultaneously will impact the ability of your team members to manage priorities and finish projects on schedule.
- *Quality.* Become aware of your own perfectionist tendencies. Learn to develop a greater tolerance for the reality of human imperfection as well as your own limitations.
- *Initiative.* Understand that often the established way of doing things is based on solid reasoning; be aware of legal and moral restrictions that may exist when implementing innovative strategies.
- *Teamwork.* Avoid a win/lose approach to people and relationships. Become more willing to share ideas and information with others in an open and accepting manner.
- *Problem-solving.* Avoid sharp criticism of others. Remain open to others' approaches to problems, even if their solutions are untested.
- *Adapting to change.* Learn to trust others more and to allow their change implementations to progress unhindered and free from judgment. Increase your awareness of the impact and consequences your behavior and actions have on the work of other people.

The initial three months of our work progressed smoothly. Leaders at every level were committed to improving all elements of their daily work while maintaining focus on the strategic objectives for that year. After the conclusion of the initial training and the implementation of the development plans, the CEO became resistant and maintained only sporadic attendance at the progress reviews. At the six-month mark of the implementation plan, the CEO completely disengaged and delegated the project to the chief operating officer.

At the end of the year, we did data comparisons on three key metrics for each department. Several departments demonstrated significant improvement in performance outcomes. The improvements were inconsistent, however, with some leaders getting significant results and other leaders maintaining previous performance levels with no significant change in outcomes. It was evident that this change initiative had lost momentum and value for the key leaders of the organization. Interviews with midlevel leaders confirmed that this change initiative was no longer a senior leader priority. The performance management system the board had requested was abandoned.

Compounding the situation, in the last three months of the implementation phase, the CEO received data on customer experience for the previous quarter. The results indicated a continuing downward trend in customer experience—the seventh straight quarter of decline. In response to these data, the CEO called a meeting of all leaders at the director level and above. The entire meeting, at which we were present, consisted of the CEO berating, belittling, and threatening to fire the entire core leadership team, complete with profanity-laced adjectives to describe the CEO's disgust and demands that results improve in the next quarter. The CEO stated that this was entirely unacceptable and that everyone present was expected to do something about it, or else they would be replaced with a new group of leaders who understood what it meant to be winners and get results.

As you might imagine, results continued to decline. The CEO held another ranting session the next quarter, and no one lost their job.

Within the next year, the CEO was forced to resign pending outcomes of an investigation into both civil and criminal wrong-doing. None of the published accounts gave any indication that this avoidable tragedy was due to a lapse of technical skill. Rather, there were specific allegations related to behavior lapses leading to decisions that violated legal and ethical boundaries, both in the organization's business practices and in the CEO's actions as its primary leader.

IMPACTS OF INEFFECTIVE LEADERSHIP BEHAVIORS

This CEO's behavior analysis profile revealed a key behavior dynamic that most likely contributed to both personal and professional ruin. This individual's leadership failures contributed to significant financial setbacks for the organization, resulting in the loss of over 300 jobs and decreasing the sustainability of the organization. Review the improvement suggestion in the Initiative performance factor of the behavior profile: "Understand that often the established way of doing things is based on solid reasoning; be aware of legal and moral restrictions that may exist when implementing innovative strategies."

The primary motivational driver for the behavior pattern of this CEO was winning. The internal focus of this leader was power and authority, and the external behavior was to focus on profit and the bottom line. When managed appropriately, all these behavior dynamics can be a positive force for performance and effective leadership. The problems for this CEO were the need to win at all costs and a lack of accountability for personal behavior. Had there been a self-imposed sense of accountability, a change of behavior would have naturally followed. The higher you climb up the corporate ladder, the more your performance and individual success depend on your behavioral capacity rather than your technical capacity.

Remember that your behavior is never confidential, is never a secret, and never lies about what you really believe or who you really are as a person and a leader. Until you conquer your inner world of thought and emotion—what you believe and what you feel—you will never conquer your outer world of behavior, which is essential to your leadership effectiveness. In the end, our undoing is not the result of a large number of behavior lapses. It only takes one or two negative behaviors repeated over and over to destroy our leadership effectiveness.

A quick search of management and leadership literature, along with our observations of leaders with whom we have worked, indicates a significant inconsistency in the ability to act on the key elements of behavior capacity—a common set of behaviors shared by highly effective leaders, regardless of gender, ethnic group, vocation, generation, or geographic location. Effective leaders of all shapes and sizes succeed in achieving results where other leaders fail because they perform at a higher level of behavioral awareness. Doing so makes them more productive and capable of achieving greater results than other leaders when faced with similar environmental variables and access to the same resources. The performance success of effective leaders is driven by a set of behaviors that enables them to

- model performance behaviors for team members,
- guide operational improvements,
- align objectives to key results,
- execute strategy consistently, and
- sustain performance improvement.

Imagine yourself as a new CEO evaluating your executive team members. Borrowing an apt question from Marshall Goldsmith (2007, 43), "Who would you rather have as a CFO? A moderately good accountant who is great with people outside the firm and skilled at managing very smart people? Or a brilliant accountant who's inept with outsiders and alienates all the smart people under him?" If we reflect honestly, we all know we want people working with us who are behaviorally smart, not just technically smart. In the end, behavior is the difference maker in organizational performance. Behavior is the difference maker in your effective leadership.

THE EFFECTIVE LEADERSHIP EQUATION

One of our main objectives is to present you with an integrated and comprehensive methodology for effective leadership development for all leaders at all levels of the organization. We believe, and the research demonstrates, that effective leaders achieve higher levels of performance results. In the expanded version of their classic book, *The Extraordinary Leader*, Zenger and Folkman (2009) demonstrated that leaders rating in the 80th percentile or higher on competency assessments produce twice the results of those in the middle range of the 60th percentile. Anderson and Adams (2016) validate this earlier research in *Mastering Leadership*, proving the connection between leadership effectiveness and performance. Their own research confirms that only two out of ten leaders are at the 80th percentile mark while six out of ten are in the middle range. When you run the math, that means that the leaders in the 80th percentile are outperforming the middle zone group by as much as 600 percent. That is an amazing difference in business results. That is why leadership effectiveness matters in efforts to achieve high levels of performance outcomes.

Senior leaders frequently tell us they believe that leadership effectiveness is essential to business outcomes and performance. Rarely do we find senior leaders putting that belief into action with an operational strategy linking development of leadership effectiveness to business processes and outcomes. Some organizations have even gone as far as trying to prove effective leadership does not matter. Scott Mautz (2019) wrote about Google's attempt to prove leadership does not matter only to discover ten key traits of the most effective leaders. Google's Project Oxygen began as an experiment with a flat organizational model with no managers. It was a spectacular failure, and Google changed direction to investigate the qualities of good leaders. The project is reminiscent of the decades-old work of Jim Collins, described in *Good to Great* (Collins 2001). Collins also set out to identify what elements contributed to the performance of top-rated companies. He did not want the answer to be effective leadership. Bowing to the power of the data, both Collins and Google altered the hypotheses of their studies and discovered a key set of behaviors that statistically improved the quality and effectiveness of leaders' performance and the overall performance of their organizations.

If you are still skeptical about the ability of effective leadership to produce high engagement and performance from your teams, we want to change your thinking. To do so, we will start with a working definition of effective leadership that relates to creating engagement, which ultimately drives performance outcomes. Here is the first of the three evidence-based equations that comprise our integrated and systematic approach to leadership development and performance management:

$$\textbf{Effective leadership} = \textit{f(x)}\ \textbf{(self-awareness)} \times \textbf{(self-management)}$$

This equation defines what we mean by effective leadership. It describes a simple relationship between a person's ability to become aware of their fundamental behavior pattern and the ability to actively and intentionally manage their behavior to create effective relationships that drive organizational performance.

You may recognize self-awareness and self-management as elements of the emotional intelligence movement initiated by Peter Salovey and John D. Mayer decades ago. Daniel Goleman became aware of their research and popularized the notion of leading with emotional intelligence in the 1990s. With the advances in neuroscience since 2010, we now have the ability to observe real-time responses from the performance-driven upper brain and the survival-driven lower brain. Consequently, we want to use this research to evolve to the next level of leadership effectiveness; namely, leading not only with emotional intelligence but also with the performance-driven upper brain. Leading with your upper brain includes being smart about your emotions. It also means learning to be smart about your behavior and leading intentionally with the upper brain, which is wired for growth, development, and achievement. To do so, we need to begin by creating conceptual understanding of key terms in our model.

Performance

Performance is fundamentally a collection of integrated behaviors moving toward a directed outcome, goal, or objective. Like behavior, then, performance is something people do, and like behavior, it is observable and measurable. Ideally, in the work setting, performance is the observable, measurable actions people take while working to align strategic objectives with key results. The actions that people take to produce performance revolve around the six leadership performance factors previously described: productivity, quality, initiative, teamwork, problem-solving, and adapting to change.

The actions associated with performance allow us to create an evidenced-based approach to leadership behavior development, using observation and measurement to discover and apply the causal connection of leadership effectiveness to team engagement and organizational performance. The study of leadership effectiveness and its ability to produce results is predicated on the understanding of how the human brain functions. The science of leadership becomes a matter of leading people's brains to higher levels of performance outcomes.

Achieving results with high-level performance is what organizations hire people to do, and to do well. This means the development of effective leadership behavior has to be aligned with objectives and expected performance outcomes. This concept runs counter to the prevailing performance appraisal model used by virtually every organization we encounter. By design, this approach is incapable of driving significant performance improvement and high-level outcomes.

Classic yet still-valid research demonstrates that individual workers have little control over any of the key measurement and performance indicators for which they are accountable on a performance appraisal (Doerr et al. 2004; Tett and Burnett 2003). Consequently, the performance measure is not truly reflective of individual behavior that links directly to the outcomes desired by leaders and actual results.

In our behavioral performance approach, organizational leaders get the results they desire by identifying key behaviors team members must demonstrate to get those results. This approach creates a shift from the leader as expert to the leader as coach. The leader has to know which behaviors produce the outcomes they desire and then focus on creating and encouraging the appropriate behavior with their team members.

This concept has hiring implications, as interviews must shift focus from technical skills to behavior skills. The desired behaviors in a new hire will be included in the job announcement in some form, perhaps under job criteria, and included in essay questions, interview questions, and other applicant screening instruments. Hiring managers will look for these behaviors during every applicant interaction.

Southwest Airlines has used this approach since the company was founded, hiring based on three key behavioral attributes, not on technical skill sets (Weber 2015). Southwest typically hires only 2 percent of prospective applicants. The primary objective of their interview process is to identify people who already behave the way they expect people to behave within the organization. Development and promotion practices also align with company values.

Additionally, when leaders focus on desirable employee behaviors, they are compelled to study the process employees use to accomplish their work objectives. One way an organization can ensure that employees get along and perform their jobs well is through the development of internal policies and procedures. The more specific the procedures, such as checklists and flowcharts that indicate decisions employees should make in the scope of their work, the easier it is for leaders to coach and develop people in the execution of those behaviors to obtain the results that leaders desire.

We are well into the twenty-first century, and amazing technology changes continue at an unabated pace. Yet the current performance management process remains outdated, ineffective, and an unpleasant burden for both leaders and team members (Di Fiore and Souza 2021). Organizations have experienced significant change in moving away from industrial worker models to knowledge-based models that include self-directed teams, virtual teams, telecommuting, home offices, and temporary workers. The COVID-19 pandemic compelled this kind of disruptive innovation by many organizations that suddenly had to manage a virtual workforce that still produced results.

The key point is that there is a direct link between results and effective leadership behavior. Effective leadership behavior creates a measurable link between the results a team produces and the team behavior that is essential to achieving the desired result. Effective leaders behave in ways that allow team members to gain great clarity about the desired outcomes of their work. Then they can create great clarity around the processes (technical capacity) necessary to get those results. Finally, effective leaders engage in the required actions and behaviors (behavior capacity) to achieve those results.

Effectiveness

Typically, we think of effectiveness in terms of evaluating performance. In assessing effectiveness, we are determining whether there is a consistent alignment among three proactive questions:

1. What did we want?
2. What did we need to do to get what we wanted?
3. Was our behavior appropriate to get us what we wanted?

When someone is taking self-directed actions to achieve a personal goal, they are accountable only to themselves and their outcomes are dictated by their behavior and by external factors. When someone has a leader and is a member of the team, evaluation of individual performance is no longer personal but collective. By *collective*, we mean that the evaluation often extends beyond factors and circumstances the individual can control. One of those factors is the leader. The individual no longer has complete autonomy to self-direct their actions. By its very nature, leadership involves an element of command and control, requiring leaders to own the performance outcomes of their teams.

In *Boundaries for Leaders*, Dr. Henry Cloud (2013, 1) describes the nature of leadership effectiveness: "Leadership is about turning a vision into reality; it's about producing real results in the real world. And that is only done through people doing what it takes to make it happen." Simply stated, when leaders identify for team members the behaviors essential to achieving the desired results, we call that effective leadership. When a situation arises and a leader needs to alter the behaviors of their team members to achieve the desired result, and those behavior changes are satisfying to both the leader and the team member, that too is the essence of effective leadership.

Effectiveness for leaders also includes controlling environmental variables that are outside the control of team members. A leader is most effective when team members can engage in their work with the least amount of disruption and distraction. Ineffective leaders, through their own behaviors, are often the source of much of this disruption and distraction. Leaders have it within their control to behave in ways that motivate their team members or contribute to a loss of motivation. Through their behavior, leaders can bring people together for a common purpose or cause divisive and unhealthy competition, creating a loss of unity that can fragment the collective performance effort of a team.

The current science demonstrates that effectiveness as a leader is not just a matter of having the right traits, such as transparency, authenticity, and empathy. These traits, and others like them, are necessary to the effectiveness of high-performing leaders, but there is something else leaders need to be effective in operational environments of increasing complexity and rapid change. Today's most effective leaders understand that their team members' engagement and performance are rooted in how those team members think, how they respond to fear in uncertainty and chaos, and how they respond to the behavior patterns of their leaders.

When leaders behave in ways that allow the brains of their team members to focus on growth, development, and achievement rather than managing fear, loss, and doubt, that is the true measure of effectiveness. When leaders can create this kind of organizational culture, they also create performance accountability, leading to measurable results that drive performance to the highest levels.

Ultimately, we can measure the effectiveness of leaders by how often they behave in ways that unify diverse groups of people. Effective leaders behave in ways that help all people find meaning, value, and purpose in their work regardless of the nature of the work itself. Finally, these leaders behave in ways that inspire and motivate people to change the world in a positive way. Leadership effectiveness is the magical elixir to create performance excellence.

Leadership

Leadership is not a solo activity. Whether you are a business leader, military leader, or civic leader, you get things done—things that really matter—through the efforts of other people. Leadership is about creating the conditions in which people's brains can work at optimal levels to produce results. We were asked in a workshop what we believe to be the most important thing a leader should be doing every day to drive performance. Here is our answer: We believe that leaders should be behaving and creating conditions for people to work in such a way that their team members show up in the morning eager to advance the goals and the objectives of the organization.

Think about what you do to lead, inspire, and influence other people. Everything you try to do as a leader is about creating a neurochemical cocktail in the brains of other people so they will behave in ways that produce results. Leadership is not just an art. Leadership is brain science that uses the elegant architecture of neural pathways and the complex interactions of cognitive brain processes to help us understand the ways we behave with one another.

Have your ever wondered why you lead people with great talent, exceptional skill, high intellect, great plans, creative vision, and clear purpose who still are not getting the results you desire? We ask this question in our leadership conferences. Here is a summary of responses we have collected over several years from leaders trying to explain this phenomenon:

- Too many competing priorities.
- Multiple and conflicting communication channels.
- Interdepartmental rivalries and unhealthy competition.
- Blame shifting and no consistent application of accountability.
- Lack of focus and fragmented effort on multiple projects.

- No consistent alignment of objectives to key results.
- Confusing activity—how busy we are—for real productivity.
- Inability to focus on the things that really matter.
- Organizational tolerance of mediocrity and poor performance.

Do any of these items sound familiar? The actual list is much longer. Note that all these items fall into the category of what we typically hear leaders call *people issues*. The skills needed to affect these issues are often called *soft skills*. Be cautious of this distinction, however, as there is nothing soft about what these dysfunctional behaviors are doing to your leadership effectiveness and organizational performance. These so-called people issues are the primary obstacles to your team members' execution of your plan because they wreak havoc with the alignment of your strategic objectives and key results.

One other point to consider is that all these dysfunctional behaviors are within your ability to control—you own them. As the leadership adage states, what you permit, you promote. The lesson here for all leaders is clear: When your behavior supports your team members' ability to focus on the things that really matter within their realm of control, it enables them to produce the results you desire as the leader.

In the end, leadership is a powerful force affecting all six leadership performance factors in a positive or negative way. Effective leadership enriches people's lives, while ineffective leadership adds to your team members' stress and burdens. Effective leadership is the firewall of protection around the hardware and operating system of an organization. Ineffective leadership is a virus disrupting the performance of the organizational software and messing with the brains of your people. You mess with the lower brains of your people at your own performance peril.

Behavior

We have substantiated the claim that individual leader behavior is the single most important predictor of a team's performance. Leadership behavior—and, specifically for our purposes, the neuroscience of leadership behavior—has many characteristics. Managing contexts is a primary consideration for leadership behavior and effectiveness. Leaders manage the process context (technical capacity) and the people context (behavior capacity) daily. The most effective leaders consistently manage both of these contexts with a set of upper brain behaviors.

We have accumulated substantial evidence from notable scholars and published in a wide variety of peer-reviewed journals that documents a hard reality: Leadership is about relationships and results. Even with all the data, the concept of behavior capacity as the dependent variable to performance, as opposed to technical skill, is still a difficult truth for many senior leaders to accept.

The science is undeniable: Nothing changes until your thinking changes. Everything can change when your thinking changes. Unless you have physiological or psychological brain impairment, your thoughts are under your control. Your thoughts are the primary driver of your emotions, and your emotions are the primary driver of your behavior. When you change your thinking, you change your behavior. When you change your behavior, you change your outcomes. This evidenced-based truth is the power of performance, and it also adds meaning, value, and purpose to your work.

BENEFITS OF CHANGE

Ineffective leadership results in staggering financial and human costs, numbering in the billions of dollars (Hougaard 2018). It is time to make a change. One of the most limiting and ineffective behaviors of leaders is refusing to change or delaying a change. In *Influential Leadership: Change Your Behavior, Change Your Organization, Change Health Care* (Frisina 2014), we wrote about the knowing and doing gap. Leaders tend to know what they need to do to change; they just delay making the change as quickly as possible. The gap between knowing what to do and actually doing it has a major impact on the quality of performance outcomes.

This principle is evident in stock market purchases. Imagine some major shift in the market. Your broker calls you and tells you it is time to buy. You hesitate, seeking more information to ensure you are making the right decision ("right" typically meaning "safe"). The reality is you most likely do not need more information; you need to trust your advisers, trust your judgment, trust prior experiences that produced effective results, and do it. Fear is always a key contributor to the knowing and doing gap. Fear is also the major driver of your lower brain.

Another disruptive behavior tendency is the need to "have everyone on board." The work of change expert John Kotter provides three typical responses to change initiatives. These responses apply to individual change as well as organizational change:

- *Get it done.* You or your team immediately understand a concept or action and are ready to execute now.
- *Skepticism.* Legitimate and well-intentioned concerns delay execution of a change initiative.
- *Resistance.* This "no way" response stops the change initiative. Ignoring this resistance is not an option, particularly when you are the immovable object.

Effective leaders have high levels of change management behavior capacity. When they discover some element of their behavior is negatively affecting the upper brain performance dynamic of their team members, they change it immediately. Change is always a fear trigger to our lower brains, but effective leaders stay focused in their upper brains and leverage change events for their own performance advantage.

There are four fundamental fear triggers:

1. Loss of control—change interferes with personal autonomy.
2. Loss of affirmation—change interferes with the way we have always done it.
3. Loss of security—change can have real pain and people can get hurt.
4. Loss of predictability—change provokes skepticism about the promised outcome (Kanter 2012).

We will explore these triggers in greater detail in part II. For now, identify your own fear trigger from this list as we move into the next chapter on self-awareness. Acknowledging your fear trigger will enable you to adjust your behavior, greatly affecting your effectiveness as a leader—but only if you are willing to change.

It is typical for highly successful people to resist changing a significant, disruptive behavior habit based on one of the known fear triggers. You cannot allow fear to keep you from changing behaviors that can become a serious liability to your leadership effectiveness and to your career. You cannot allow your current level of success to keep you from changing either.

Executive coach Marshall Goldsmith has identified one of the greatest mistakes successful people make when it comes to changing a disruptive behavior: the false assumption that "I am successful. This is how I behave. Therefore, I must be successful *because* I behave this way." Our challenge is helping you see that sometimes leaders are successful *despite* their behavior. Remember that behavioral lapses are perfectly obvious to everyone except the person committing them.

KEY TAKEAWAYS

- Your behavior, manifested by your brain activity—thoughts, perceptions, mental judgments, and emotions—is a catalyst altering the nature and effectiveness of your personal and professional relationships.

- Just as one steel ball of Newton's cradle collides with the other balls and creates a predictable outcome, so too our behavior as leaders collides with the brains of our team members, with equally predictable results.

- The truth about performance is that your technical skills never go any higher than your behavior capacity to create highly effective relationships that drive performance.

- Effective leaders of all types succeed in achieving results where other leaders fail because they perform at a higher level of behavioral awareness.

- By its very nature, leadership has an element of command and control, and leaders have to own their teams' performance.

- When your behavior supports your team members' ability to focus and get clarity on the things that really matter within their realm of control, it affects their ability to produce the results you desire as the leader.

- In the end, leadership is a powerful force influencing all six leadership performance factors in a positive or negative way.

PUT IT TO WORK

1. Do you have a way to compare the leadership effectiveness of the key leaders of your organization? Do you have a way to compare leadership effectiveness in your organization with that of your primary competitors?

2. Do you have a way to measure your leadership effectiveness as a means of leveraging your organizational performance?

3. What about the way you show up as a leader affects the engagement and performance of your team? Would you follow you as a leader?

4. Do you know how you are "showing up" to your team members?

    - How do your team members experience your physical and emotional energy?

    - Do you ever listen to yourself talk? How do you sound to others? Is your communication positive or negative, encouraging or discouraging, approachable or unapproachable, in terms of both what you say and how you behave?

5. What is one thing you could change—stop doing or start doing—that would greatly increase your level of leadership influence and effectiveness and improve the quality of an important relationship? Once you identify the one thing, are you willing to do it? If not, ask yourself why not.

REFERENCES

Anderson, R., and W. Adams. 2016. *Mastering Leadership: An Integrated Framework for Breakthrough Performance and Extraordinary Business Results*. Hoboken, NJ: Wiley & Sons.

Cloud, H. 2013. *Boundaries for Leaders: Results, Relationships, and Being Ridiculously in Charge*. New York: HarperCollins.

Collins, J. 2001. *Good to Great: Why Some Companies Make the Leap and Others Don't*. New York: HarperCollins.

Di Fiore, A., and M. Souza. 2021. "Are Peer Reviews the Future of Performance Evaluations?" *Harvard Business Review*. Published January 12. https://hbr.org/2021/01/are-peer-reviews-the-future-of-performance-evaluations.

Doerr, K., T. Freed, T. Mitchell, C. Schriesheim, and X. Zhou. 2004. "Work Flow Policy and Within-Worker and Between-Workers Variability in Performance." *Journal of Applied Psychology* 89 (5): 911–21.

Frisina, M. E. 2014. *Influential Leadership: Change Your Behavior, Change Your Organization, Change Healthcare*. Chicago: Health Administration Press.

Goldsmith, M. 2007. *What Got You Here Won't Get You There: How Successful People Become Even More Successful*. New York: Hyperion.

Hamilton, S. 2010. *Profiles Performance Indicator Technical Manual*. Waco, TX: Profiles International.

Hougaard, R. 2018. "The Real Crisis in Leadership." *Forbes*. Published September 9. www.forbes.com/sites/rasmushougaard/2018/09/09/the-real-crisis-in-leadership/.

Kanter, R. 2012. "Ten Reasons People Resist Change." *Harvard Business Review*. Published September 25. https://hbr.org/2012/09/ten-reasons-people-resist-chang.

Mautz, S. 2019. "Google Tried to Prove Managers Don't Matter. Instead, It Discovered 10 Traits of the Very Best Ones." *Inc.* Published June 5. www.inc.com/scott-mautz/google-tried-to-prove-managers-dont-matter-instead-they-discovered-10-traits-of-very-best-ones.html.

Tett, R., and D. Burnett. 2003. "A Personality Trait–Based Interactionist Model of Job Performance." *Journal of Applied Psychology* 88 (3): 500–17.

Weber, J. 2015. "How Southwest Airlines Hires Such Dedicated People." *Harvard Business Review*. Published December 2. https://hbr.org/2015/12/how-southwest-airlines-hires-such-dedicated-people.

Zenger, J., and J. Folkman. 2009. *The Extraordinary Leader: Turning Good Managers into Great Leaders*. New York: McGraw Hill.

CHAPTER 2

Self-Awareness

*The difference between who you are and what you want
to be is what you do.*

—Charles Duhigg

WE HAVE ALWAYS considered self-awareness to be a fundamental behavior trait of influential and highly effective leaders. Highly successful organizations distinguish themselves with leaders who have a heightened sense of self-awareness. Sadly, far too many leaders are the exact opposite. They unconsciously mess with the upper brains of their peers and team members, disrupting performance behaviors. They are unaware of how their ineffective leadership behavior negatively affects the ability of peers and team members to gain clarity of purpose, maintain focus on daily work routines, and stay connected to the part of their brain that allows for personal growth, professional achievement, and high levels of performance outcomes.

By learning and practicing self-awareness, leaders become comfortable with their internal thought processes, values, beliefs, preferences, attitudes, and emotions. They become self-managers, careful about how they present themselves to others and how they respond to external events. Consequently, a self-aware leader is in a better position to collaborate and connect with others, increasing both influence in relationships and effectiveness in achieving results.

Consider the case of a CEO of a midsize healthcare system. This executive was a high achiever and successful throughout her career until she became the system CEO. Two years into her tenure, the board of directors requested an employee engagement survey based on input that, despite promising performance numbers, morale was low and top-performing members of the organization were threatening to leave, including some physicians. As in the cases in chapter 1, no one doubted the CEO's technical skill capacity. She had a master's degree in health administration from a top program and had excelled in all her previous management positions. Financials improved during the early stages of her tenure. Everyone agreed that she was getting all the right numbers and had a clear strategy for organizational growth. Everyone also agreed that people did not like working for her. One exit interview comment read, "During a performance appraisal, she said, 'I will always get all the credit when things go well, and you will always get all the blame when things go wrong.' It was at that point I realized it was time for me to go."

We can acquire a host of bad habits in our personal and professional behaviors. One of the worst is claiming credit for the work of others. Not only does this behavior demonstrate a lack of recognition of the work of others, but it also serves as a theft of the intellectual property and effort of another person. Even the most developed human being is going to have a lower brain response of negative emotion, manifesting in bitterness, resentment, and in some cases outright hatred for a leader who behaves in such a selfish manner.

This type of behavior compounds financial, performance, and human losses. When leaders behave in ways that are contrary to the core values of the organization without facing any consequences, the resulting moral injury affects the performance and retention of team members. Psychiatrist Jonathan Shay (2014, 183) coined the term *moral injury* for this behavior, defined as "a betrayal of what's right by someone who holds legitimate authority . . . in a high stakes situation."

Do not think that this kind of behavior lapse is rare among top-level executive leaders (Patel 2017). A common trait of highly successful people is their insensitivity to the efforts of others. The tendency when climbing the proverbial ladder is to become self-centered. Successful people get used to talking in terms of their own accomplishments: *my* career, *my* performance, *my* promotions, and *my* needs. They wire their brains into a pattern of thinking that puts the self before others. These leaders walk a fine line between ethical and unethical behavior. They can disrespect their team members with rude behaviors such as being late for meetings, using a smartphone during conversations, raising their voices in anger, and interrupting in the middle of presentations (Magee et al. 2005). Research on incivility in the workplace clearly demonstrates that leaders who behave badly do so because they believe their behavior is justified simply because they are the boss (Taylor et al. 2019).

As you might imagine, the employee engagement survey was not very complimentary of this CEO's behavior profile. In her meteoric rise to the C-suite, she developed a major disconnect between her internal reality (internal self-awareness) and her understanding of how her behavior was affecting other people (external self-awareness). Her unwillingness to accept suggestions for improving her effectiveness and changing her behavior eventually resulted in her being fired from the organization. With all her years of technical training, her management education, her professional development, her career advancement, despite her ability to get results, she had never addressed two fundamental questions about leadership: (1) What does it mean to be a highly effective leader? and (2) What behavioral changes do I need to make to become one?

Developing self-awareness requires time, effort, practice, and a focused commitment. Once developed and practiced regularly, self-awareness enables you to manage your behavior, improve your personal and professional relationships, and create and sustain your leadership effectiveness. Many leaders are reluctant to become self-aware because they resist a key element of personal growth—feedback from the people around them.

Self-awareness is not just an internal self-examination exercise. Completing a personality assessment to discover the "real you" has no correlation to improving performance and leadership effectiveness. There is value in seeking to understand and align the elements of the inner self, of course. This process, which the research literature calls *internal self-awareness,* is clearly one aspect of performance behavior self-awareness (Eurich 2018a). Rarely in our executive coaching do we encounter a leader who resists our help in discovering their inner self.

By itself, however, internal self-awareness is insufficient for confronting complex leadership challenges. Connecting and engaging with team members in a positive and productive way requires more; it requires paying attention to how our behavior positively or negatively affects people—what the research literature calls *external self-awareness.* Exhibit 2.1 depicts the dual nature of self-awareness.

Research by psychologists J. Gregory Hixon and William Swann (1993) demonstrates a greater resistance to learning and changing when people are asked to develop external self-awareness. Feedback about the behavior traits of likability and sociability created contrasting behaviors from participants in their study. The research participants who thought about why they were the way they were and considered their impact on other people showed an increased denial of feedback. Participants who were asked to focus on the question "What kind of person do I want to be?" willingly accepted the feedback and the learning opportunity. The "What do I need to do to get better?" mindset is the gateway to candid self-awareness and the hallmark of highly effective leaders. The adage on feedback now has science to support it: People who don't want to change don't want feedback, and none of us wants to offer it to them either.

Exhibit 2.1 Internal and External Self-Awareness

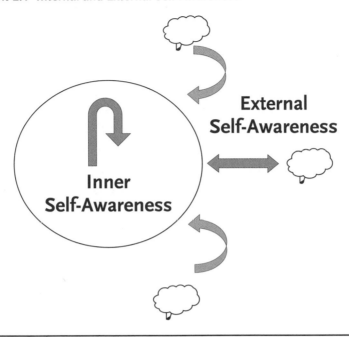

The knowledge of self-awareness (both internal and external), and its development as a behavior performance strategy, comes down to a simple question: Do you want to get better as a leader? Leaders who focus on learning about the inner self and are willing to pay attention to how others perceive their external self will achieve the greatest level of self-awareness. In turn, these leaders will have the greatest opportunity to expand their leadership effectiveness and drive performance outcomes to the highest levels.

THE DISCOVERY OF SELF-AWARENESS

Self-awareness is the starting point of effective leadership. Becoming aware of our thoughts, emotions, and behavior is indispensable to becoming a highly effective leader. Until we learn to conquer our inner world and its related performance triad—the cognitive triangle—we will never be able to fully conquer our outside world and the impact our behavior has on the people who matter most to us, personally and professionally.

The importance of self-awareness to leadership effectiveness follows a simple premise—to lead others effectively, we must first lead ourselves effectively. This prompts the question of when all this interest in self-awareness began. One of the earliest examples comes from Aristotle, who would compare the behaviors of people and apply some moral standard to those behaviors. Aristotle's conception of self-awareness sprang from his notion of the "four causes" used to define what makes something what it is (Hocutt 1974). The first of Aristotle's four causes is the material cause—for human beings, our physical makeup of flesh, bones, and blood. We can expand this concept to thoughts and emotions—the mental building blocks, as it were, of what makes you, you.

Centuries later, Benjamin Franklin also took an interest in the concept of self-awareness as a way of becoming a better human being. He used journaling to capture information and data about his behavior on a daily basis. He became a student of social science, using himself as his research subject. Franklin's curiosity and achievements in a wide array of professional pursuits allowed him enough wealth to retire in his forties. In his autobiography (which you should include on your reading list), Franklin attributes much of his success to the practice of 13 core life behaviors (Franklin [1793] 1993).

Franklin set out on this bold pursuit of moral perfection when he was 20, identifying a list of core values to guide his conduct and behavior. He resolved to avoid any wrongdoing and created a system to track his progress and ensure accountability in his pursuit of moral excellence. Franklin's autobiography includes an account of how this list evolved (Gunn 2017):

> My list of virtues contained at first but twelve; but a
> Quaker friend having kindly informed me that I was gener-
> ally thought proud; that my pride show'd itself frequently

in conversation; that I was not content with being in the right when discussing any point, but was overbearing, and rather insolent, of which he convinced me by mentioning several instances; I determined endeavoring to cure myself, if I could, of this vice or folly among the rest, and I added Humility to my list.

We find it remarkable that humility found its way to the top of Jim Collins's list of "Level 5" leader behavior attributes in his book *Good to Great* (Collins 2001). We find it noteworthy as well that Franklin's ability to achieve this level of self-awareness came from his willingness to accept direct feedback from others about how they experienced him and his behavior. Finally, we find it distressing that a lack of humility, demonstrated in the inability to accept feedback about how our ineffective leadership behavior affects others, is still derailing executive careers today.

What happens when someone lacks self-awareness—especially in the context of aligning strategic objectives with key results in business performance? What do you believe about self-awareness and its scientific link to highly effective leadership behavior that gets results? Can you see how self-awareness drives effective leadership, and how that leadership is vital to transforming the workplace culture to allow people to discover meaning, value, and purpose? Now might be a good time for you to reflect on these questions.

A DEFINITION FOR SELF-AWARENESS THEORY

The *APA Dictionary of Psychology* (2021) defines self-awareness as "self-focused attention or knowledge." As a leadership skill, self-awareness means being attentive, focused, and alert to your thoughts, emotions, and behaviors as you engage executive skills to achieve peak performance outcomes. Leaders who practice self-awareness have increased cognitive functions, improved memory, a higher level of emotional regulation, and a stronger immune system (Miller 2021). More importantly, practitioners of self-awareness learn to connect and ignite the upper brain, the prefrontal cortex, which is built for growth, achievement, and performance. When connected to their upper brain, self-aware leaders adjust their perceptions of reality, increasing their leadership effectiveness even when faced with the most challenging circumstances. They also create the same effect in the brains of their peers and team members, leading those people's upper brains to higher levels of performance outcomes and personal achievement.

In the late 1800s, William James made a distinction between the subjective and objective self. Since then, self-awareness has become the focus of many psychologists. Research by Shelley Duval and Robert Wicklund (1972) formed the basis of the contemporary study of self-awareness generally and objective self-awareness specifically. Their work demonstrated that empirical study of self-focused attention was possible. They asserted that at any given moment a person could be both self-focused and other-focused. This startling revelation provides an evidenced-based approach to understanding why we have egocentric leaders and servant leaders, why we have focused leaders and unfocused leaders, why we have process-oriented leaders and people-oriented leaders, and why some leaders have a high degree of emotional regulation and other leaders are volatile and emotionally unpredictable.

By using self-awareness to manage thoughts, emotions, and behaviors, leaders can learn to control the executive functions of their upper brains, minimizing the distraction and fear responses of the lower brain's limbic system. Both the prefrontal cortex and the limbic system are associated with predictable behaviors. This neuroscience is the key to creating a leader's behavior performance profile. Once they know their own behavior tendencies, leaders can effectively lead themselves and others with shared goals and objectives—what we call learning to lead with the upper brain. The cascading effect on performance is illustrated in the leadership effectiveness equations (exhibit 0.2 in the introduction): Leaders who use self-awareness as a performance strategy lead their own brains effectively, and are capable of leading the brains of other people to higher levels of engagement. Both factors make these leaders more capable of leading complex organizations to higher levels of performance outcomes.

Like Aristotle, Franklin, and William James before them, Duval and Wicklund believed that inward focus involved comparing the self with objective standards. These standards arise from interactions with the environment. Once these comparisons are internalized, the individual may adjust their thoughts and behaviors. The more self-focused a person is, the more self-aware the person becomes. The work to define when self-awareness emerges, why it is important, and what it means to our human development is still ongoing. What is most important is the opportunity to apply neuroscience research to individual peak performance and determine the effective leadership behaviors that alter business performance outcomes.

A well-publicized example of self-awareness applied to leadership effectiveness and team performance emerged in 2014. Pete Carroll, head coach of the National Football League's Seattle Seahawks, had become the focus of media attention created by the transformation of the Seattle franchise (Boyce 2014). The fascination was not only that Seattle was winning a lot of football games and contending for the Super Bowl, but also that the players themselves were transforming. What was the root cause of these rapid and significant changes? The answer was self-awareness.

Pete Carroll brought a change in traditional leadership philosophy to Seattle. He hired a mindset coach, Michael Gervais, who crafted a coaching style and leadership philosophy with Carroll that emphasized mindset training. One of Carroll's team goals was developing well-rounded people, not just great athletes. He wanted players to translate what they were doing to achieve performance excellence on the football field into their personal lives as well. He asked players to become self-aware and to discover their authentic inner selves. Through that discovery, as Gervais coached them, they could then focus on what was possible in the world around them and perform in ways that turned those possibilities into realities. Today, many people use the cliché "becoming the best version of myself" to describe the use of this human performance methodology. There is miraculous, life-changing power in the daily practice of self-awareness principles.

There have been many changes since 2014. Once considered a novelty among positive-thinking and self-help advocates, the growth of neuroscience and the development of technologies such as functional magnetic resonance imaging provide a scientific basis for understanding the behavior of our brains. We can integrate this new understanding in our business coaching practices and daily leadership behaviors to align strategic objectives with producing key results. We also can help people discover meaning, value, and purpose in their work. Doing so creates engagement, and that engagement drives organizational performance. Resisting a science-based approach to leadership effectiveness is bad for people and bad for business. There are tangible consequences for leaders who ignore the practice of self-awareness; they do so at their own performance peril.

CONSEQUENCES OF LOW SELF-AWARENESS

Self-awareness is critical to effective leadership because it allows us to actively manage the parts of our brain that regulate thoughts and emotions. When we allow the upper and lower brain to run on autopilot, beyond our conscious reach, we cannot use executive skill sets to formulate functional strategies, identify key objectives, and align those objectives to achieve key results. As mentioned previously, we can think about thoughts, emotions, and behaviors in cause-and-effect relationships. This cognitive triangle is often depicted in a popular diagram (shown in exhibit 2.2) used in the cognitive behavioral therapy (CBT) model.

CBT is a validated collection of practical techniques for managing emotions and changing detrimental, unproductive, and disruptive behaviors. CBT typically employs a combination of

Exhibit 2.2 The Cognitive Triangle

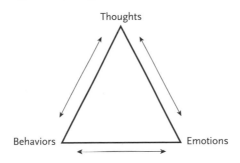

self-awareness, critical analysis through journaling exercises, and taking actions toward goal-oriented change. More than an effective treatment for mental illness, CBT is an approach almost anyone can use to gain greater mental clarity, align goals and objectives with key results, and improve quality of life.

CBT helps answer a few fundamental questions: What do I want (the goal)? What am I doing in my behavior that is not getting me what I want? What behavioral changes will help me achieve my goal? CBT creates clarity by linking productive thoughts, emotions, and behaviors to the creation of a development plan for self-improvement; when executed consistently over time, CBT produces higher levels of performance outcomes.

Often, we go through our daily routines on autopilot—feeling emotions, thinking automatic thoughts, and reacting with behaviors based on those automatic thoughts without being fully aware of how our behaviors are influencing others and ourselves. This can be extremely problematic in the workplace if our thoughts, feelings, and behaviors are particularly negative or destructive to others. The great news is that we do not have to get stuck on autopilot. We do not have to keep going through life exhibiting destructive and unproductive behaviors. Neuroscientists have discovered that we can rewire our brains, literally changing their structure through training techniques. Self-awareness is one of those key training techniques, if you are willing to learn it and apply it to improve your leadership effectiveness.

Even with the mounting evidence that self-awareness is important for job performance, career success, and leadership effectiveness, it is still a neglected performance strategy in today's workplace and rarely visible in actual practice. In one five-year study, although 95 percent of study participants thought they were self-aware, only 10–15 percent actually were (Eurich 2018b). These "un-self-aware" leaders and colleagues are responsible for a range of negative consequences and behaviors:

- Decreased motivation among team members.
- Increased turnover and reduced retention among high performers.
- Increased stress, which disrupts communication and other key aspects of functional interpersonal relationships.
- Reduced productivity (by as much as 50 percent).
- Refusal to listen to and accept supportive feedback.
- Lack of accountability and shifting of blame for poor performance to others.
- Lack of empathy and compassion for the needs of others.

Leaders may derail their careers because they lack the key behavioral skills needed for success. The lack of intelligence, operational skill, critical reasoning ability, and talent is rarely the cause of failure. More often, it is because of the undesirable qualities of bad judgment, an inability to build a high-performing team, a failure to relate well to others, and an inability or unwillingness to learn from behavior lapses and mistakes.

Ineffective leadership is costly to all of us. It damages staff morale, organizational productivity, and the bottom line. We are advocating a radical shift in leadership strategy, from one that focuses on technical elements and processes to one that considers the impact of poor behavior on safety, quality, and for healthcare, patient experience. This change must start with leaders at all levels. Real change will never come from outside consultants or the latest management fad. It will come from within an organization, once its leaders understand the power of leadership effectiveness to transform an organization and have the will and desire to do so.

DEVELOPING SELF-AWARENESS

Human beings are intrinsically designed to learn, grow, and connect with others. This human tendency is particularly apparent in the workplace. Most of us want to create close bonds with colleagues in the mutual pursuit of meaning, value, and purpose in our lives. This ability to connect well with others is essential to the concept of engagement—showing up at work to further the goals and objectives of the organization.

Where does engagement start? Leaders set the example by creating the conditions necessary to drive human performance. Individual leader behavior is the single most important predictor of team performance. Leaders who seek to develop the greatness of others achieve the greatest amount of leadership effectiveness for the overall benefit of the organization. Developing and applying self-awareness is the critical component of that effectiveness.

Learning and practicing self-awareness has two essential elements—regulating your thoughts and regulating your emotions. Just as we can use behavior training to develop skills or exercise our brains to improve cognitive functions, we can also train our brains to regulate thoughts and emotions. Regulating thoughts and emotions in a positive and productive way allows us to connect and ignite our upper brain for growth, achievement, and performance. When we yield to fear impulses and react to external threats, the lower brain can override the activation and normal function of the upper brain.

While managing responses to threat, fear, and anxiety, the lower brain can literally block access to the executive skill sets of the upper brain. Survival drive undermines performance drive in the brain every time. This entire process starts with thoughts. Our thoughts determine how we interpret the world in which we live. Negative thoughts not only influence our behaviors, but also cause actual physical and emotional damage.

Neuroanatomist Pierre Paul Broca first used the term *limbic system* to describe a collection of brain structures that are involved in emotional regulation (Birn et al. 2014). The amygdala is a part of the limbic system and is fundamentally responsible for responding to fear stimuli. The human brain has a remarkable capacity for growth, achievement, and performance. It also has a remarkable capacity for instinctive responses to threat stimuli to help us survive. As remarkable as the human brain is, it cannot perform both thriving and surviving functions at the same time. Consequently, we must learn to recognize and understand when survival instincts are appropriate and helpful and when they are damaging and disruptive. By regulating thought and emotion through self-awareness, we build the behavior capacity to create effective relationships and increase organizational performance.

As you may know, brain functions are largely localized to certain areas of the left and right hemispheres. Typically, each lobe of each hemisphere is concerned with specific processes. Knowing this, we can explain leadership effectiveness using brain science. A specific part of the brain regulates executive skill sets. Another part of the brain regulates response to threats and survival. These two functions can compete for our time and attention. Therefore, we must train the brain to respond appropriately to external stimuli and manage toxic thoughts and disruptive emotions to achieve high levels of human performance and leadership effectiveness.

Regulating Your Thoughts

Learning to regulate your thoughts is the starting point of self-awareness and peak upper brain performance. Your awareness of positive and negative thoughts and your ability to regulate your thought processes are fundamental to your ability to manage your emotions and behavior effectively as a leader. Remember, thoughts are real, physical things that occupy physical space in the brain. Every day, you alter the physical structure of your brain through your thoughts. When you objectively observe your thought patterns and mindsets, you gain the ability to identify and eliminate negative thinking that blocks the performance of your upper brain. By engaging in this process purposefully, multiple times a day, you begin to rewire your brain for growth, development, and achievement by choosing positive thoughts. In neuroscience, the saying is, "Brain cells that fire together, wire together." Nothing in our lives changes until our thinking changes. Your brain cells physically react to your thinking. What you wire into your brain through your thinking gets stored in your nonconscious mind. Nearly every thought we have is stored in the nonconscious mind and affects our emotions and behavior.

The nonconscious mind informs our perceptions and emotions during encounters with new external stimuli, directing what we say and what we do. In the physical world, a person's ability to control the cause-and-effect relationships between thought, emotion, and behavior determines every resulting consequence. This reality has tremendous implications for the choices leaders make every day to create engagement for their team members and drive their organization's performance.

Leaders need to see themselves as guardians of the thinking process for themselves individually and for their teams collectively. The prevailing thought patterns of a leader, a team, and an entire organization will dictate the level of their performance outcomes. There are a host of self-limiting thinking traps messing with the performance of leaders' brains. We hold all kinds of personal and professional thoughts and beliefs, and they have a direct influence on what we achieve. When we have empowering thoughts, our achievements can feel almost effortless. When we have self-limiting and negative thoughts, however, we can feel like the mythical Greek king Sisyphus, repeatedly pushing a boulder up a steep hill only to watch it roll back down again. We can take steps to end this cycle of destructive thinking, however.

One of the primary techniques to help you regulate your own thoughts, function as the guardian of your team's collective thinking, and increase your leadership effectiveness is to practice mindfulness. Mindfulness is nothing more than learning to think about and focus full attention on what you are thinking. It is a technique of calming your mind, reducing stress, increasing focus, reducing distraction, avoiding multitasking, eliminating disruptive behaviors, and being mentally and physically present with people. Mindfulness is a means of improving your leadership effectiveness and overall well-being in every aspect of your daily work life. The practice of thinking about your thinking is at least as old as the biblical proverb: As you think in your heart—what you think about in your inner world—so you will become in your behavior—what you do in the outer world.

Remember that your behavior is never private. Your behavior is never confidential. Your behavior reveals what you believe to be true in your heart. Your behavior dictates your leadership effectiveness.

Unfortunately, the practice of mindfulness evokes negative connotations for many leaders. We urge you to separate yourself from any preconceived notions and judgments you might have about mindfulness. Keep an open mind and give us a chance to present you with a neuroscience-based approach to some fundamental mindfulness practices guaranteed to improve your leadership effectiveness.

In clinical trials, the Mayo Clinic (2020) identified key aspects of inefficient work practices that are aggravated by increased stress:

- Overanalysis and overplanning
- Fragmented and ineffective problem-solving
- Loss of focus and daydreaming

- Negativity during meetings
- Increased anxiety, signs of emotional distress, and symptoms of depression

The researchers found that practicing mindfulness eased stress, anxiety, pain, depression, insomnia, and hypertension (high blood pressure). Primarily, mindfulness can help you regulate your thoughts with greater balance and acceptance, exhibiting behaviors that are the most effective for you to achieve your goals and objectives at a higher level of human performance. The science clearly demonstrates that mindfulness can

- improve attention and focus;
- increase engagement and decrease aspects of job burnout; and
- improve sleep, increasing the mental and physical energy available for performance.

The resources for developing mindfulness habits are readily available. Mindfulness has been a staple of positive psychology since the establishment of the field—not so much linked to positive psychology as fundamental to its very nature. The close ties between mindfulness and positive psychology make sense when you consider the outcomes of mindfulness: increased positivity, a greater sense of coherence, better quality of life, increased empathy, more satisfying relationships, and increased hope (Vago and Silbersweig 2012). Some common mindfulness techniques you can learn and practice include the following:

- Take a ten-minute pause periodically throughout your day to slow your thinking.
- Do breathing exercises to help keep you calm and regulate your heartbeat.

- Take time to think about your thinking, using prayer, meditation, or both to capture key thoughts occupying your mind.

We do not intend to repeat all the specifics of developing a mindfulness practice here. Our purpose is to help you understand that without mindfulness you cannot control your thoughts. Exercising discipline in your thinking will bring your thoughts under your direct and conscious control. Doing so is the first step in learning to lead from your upper brain and improve your leadership effectiveness. It will also provide the added benefit of living a more joyful and grateful life in a complex and chaotic world.

When you make a conscious effort to focus your attention on your thoughts—to think about what you are thinking—you stimulate a variety of brain chemicals called neurotransmitters that begin to change the physical structure of your brain. This means you can create the ability to distinguish between positive thoughts and negative thoughts. You can choose to retain the positive thoughts and reject the negative ones. By being intentional about what you choose to think, you can control your brain's sensory processing capacity (Leaf 2013).

Research demonstrates that 5 to 15 minutes a day of focused attention on what you are thinking enhances your ability to think critically, problem solve, and improve interpersonal relationships. Mindfulness practice can stimulate development of three primary factors for leading effectively in the twenty-first century: creating resilience, managing situations of increasing complexity, and increasing collaboration. The powerful outcomes created by consistent mindfulness practice have staggering implications for future leadership development and business performance.

Mindfulness is a teachable skill and a practical tool, and should be an essential component of any leadership development program. Regulating your thoughts is essential for leading from your upper brain and controlling the disruptive elements of your lower brain. Mindfulness training has specific applications to helping leaders and team members maintain alignment between performance objectives and key results. These skills improve leadership effectiveness and increase your team's engagement. Mindfulness will help you thrive as a leader, create an organization that people value, and improve your overall quality of life. As Daniel Goleman, Richard Boyatzis, and Annie McKee (2013) wrote, "Ultimately, the most meaningful act of responsibility that leaders can do is to control their own state of mind."

We cannot overstate the need for leaders to be able to understand and respond appropriately to business decisions that directly affect desired outcomes. To be an effective leader and manage all your responsibilities at a high level of performance outcomes, you must learn to lead with your upper brain.

Regulating Your Emotions

Self-awareness means having a deep understanding of regulating our emotions as well as our thoughts. As previously discussed, aspiring effective leaders cannot allow disruptive and negative thoughts, loss of focus and attention, and fear of decisive decision-making to control their behavior. Similarly, effective leaders cannot allow disruptive emotions such as fear, rage, and contempt to control their behavior either. Emotionally negative stimuli can be overpowering; these impulses are the brain's way of telling us we might be in danger. These lower brain emotions create neurophysiological and neurochemical triggers that can block the upper brain from focusing on in-the-moment technical skill functions and tasks. Learning emotional regulation allows leaders and their team members to manage this disruption in a way that keeps them connected to their upper brains, allowing them to maintain a high level of performance outcomes.

Perhaps the most dramatic example of the need to regulate emotions comes from a phenomenon referred to as psychosomatic death. Have you ever been in a haunted house or on a death-defying roller coaster? Have you ever bungee jumped or forgotten about a math exam? Our lives can be filled with high-stress experiences, both intentional and unplanned. No doubt you have a memory of a stressful experience that prompted the response, "That scared me to death." Psychosomatic death describes those cases where an emotional response was so extreme that it actually did cause a person's death (Samuels 2007).

Although the concept of emotional regulation is difficult to capture with an objective definition, a vast amount of informative research is available on the topic. While fear and stress response in the workplace may not be so intense as to cause a psychosomatic death, the disruption of cognitive functions is such that performance suffers dramatically. Long-term stress exposure has negative consequences for the physical health of the brain and the overall mental health of the individual. Any technique that decreases the stress response is beneficial for increasing leadership effectiveness. How leaders regulate emotion is critical to whether their teams' performance outcomes are positive or negative. Again, while we are not providing an exhaustive list of brain training techniques, we want to discuss one of the most successful strategies you can use in managing your emotions—reappraisal, or reframing (Thompson 1994).

In simple terms, reappraisal is a thinking process that involves reinterpreting an external event to increase or decrease your emotional response to the event. If you are experiencing a negative emotion, then you change your thinking about how you are interpreting the event. When you change your thinking, you change the emotion. The process of reappraisal can work in either a positive or negative direction, which is why thought regulation is so important. If you think about a specific event in negative terms, then you create negative emotions. Conversely, when you think and interpret an event in a positive way, you create positive emotions. Your emotions help inform your thinking. Reappraisal is a way to reframe an event so you can change your emotional response.

A classic example is how we respond to a difficult boss or team member. Rather than allowing your mind to jump from one negative thought to another, you can imagine what you can learn by working with difficult people. You can also use empathy to consider what difficulties and challenges might exist in this person's life that make their behavior so disruptive. You might ask yourself what difficult situation is affecting your boss right now or how you might see the situation from the other person's perspective. How would you respond if you were walking in their shoes? You could also benefit from telling yourself, "It's OK to feel anxious or overwhelmed; it's a normal response."

Using reappraisal as a strategy for regulating emotions has substantial research support. Reappraisal also requires practice, and requires you to adopt a certain perspective about life and work. Baseball legend Babe Ruth struck out more than three times as often as he hit home runs. Even the most talented baseball players have a failure rate at bat of about three to one. As many great thought leaders have said, it is all a matter of perspective. Babe Ruth is reported to have said, "Every strike brings me closer to the next home run." What is your perspective? Are you seeing failure or opportunity? Are you giving in to fear or seeking to discover something new? The most critical aspect of your leadership effectiveness is how you choose to respond to the external events you encounter daily, so choose wisely.

Of all the techniques necessary for attaining self-awareness, regulating your thoughts and emotions is the most important skill you can acquire on your way to becoming an effective leader.

KEY TAKEAWAYS

- Highly successful organizations distinguish themselves with leaders who have a heightened sense of self-awareness.
- A self-aware leader is in a better position to collaborate and connect with others, increasing both their influence in relationships and their effectiveness in achieving results.

- Leaders who focus on learning about the inner self and are willing to pay attention to how others perceive their external self will achieve the greatest level of self-awareness and have the greatest opportunity to expand their leadership effectiveness.

- Leaders need to see themselves as guardians of the collective thinking process of their teams.

- Mindfulness is nothing more than learning to think about and focus full attention on what you are thinking.

- Emotional regulation is a skill that allows leaders and their team members to manage disruption in a way that enables them to stay connected to their upper brain, thereby maintaining a high level of performance outcomes.

PUT IT TO WORK

For the first two questions, you may find the free self-examination at Mind Tools helpful ("How Emotionally Intelligent Are You?" www.mindtools.com/pages/article/ei-quiz.htm).

1. Do you know what behaviors you display on a daily basis?

2. Are your habits bringing you closer to or pulling you away from achieving the high levels of performance necessary to make a significant difference in people's lives?

3. Describe your understanding of self-awareness. Do you believe you are self-aware? If so, how do you maintain this awareness?

4. Many feedback tools are available, with varying degrees of effectiveness and practicality. Regardless of which system you use, do not lose sight of its purpose: to provide feedback and diligently apply the lessons learned. By doing this, we can move from complacency, fear, and doubt to improved behavior, creative thought processes,

mental toughness, and discipline—all of which help us to shape or recreate our lives and increase leadership effectiveness.

5. What are you experiencing through your five senses as you are reading this sentence? Record your observations in as much detail as possible. This exercise will demonstrate to you how random your thought processes can be. It will help you become more aware of what you are allowing to come into your mind.

6. Now read what you wrote in response to the previous question. See if you can identify any attitude or emotion reflected in your thinking. Group your responses into categories: (1) positive or negative, and (2) in your control or out of your control. Once you have your list, focus on only those thoughts that are positive and in your control. Let go of everything else.

REFERENCES

APA Dictionary of Psychology. 2021. "Self-Awareness." Accessed August 31. https://dictionary.apa.org/self-awareness.

Birn, R., A. Shackman, J. Oler, L. Williams, D. McFarlin, G. Rogers, S. Shelton, A. Alexander, D. Pine, M. Slattery, R. Davidson, A. Fox, and N. Kalin. 2014. "Evolutionarily Conserved Prefrontal-Amygdalar Dysfunction in Early-Life Anxiety." *Molecular Psychiatry* 19 (8): 915–22.

Boyce, B. 2014. "How Coach Pete Carroll Is Changing NFL Culture." *Mindful*. Published December 24. www.mindful.org/how-coach-pete-carroll-is-changing-nfl-culture/.

Collins, J. 2001. *Good to Great: Why Some Companies Make the Leap and Others Don't*. New York: HarperCollins.

Duval, S., and R. Wicklund. 1972. *A Theory of Objective Self-Aware-ness*. Oxford, UK: Oxford Press.

Eurich, T. 2018a. "What Self-Awareness Really Is (and How to Cultivate It)." *Harvard Business Review*. Published January 4. https://hbr.org/2018/01/what-self-awareness-really-is-and-how-to-cultivate-it.

———. 2018b. "Working with People Who Aren't Self-Aware." *Harvard Business Review*. Published October 19. https://hbr.org/2018/10/working-with-people-who-arent-self-aware.

Franklin, B. (1793) 1993. *The Autobiography of Benjamin Franklin*. Edited by L. P. Masur. Boston: Bedford/St. Martin's.

Goleman, D., R. Boyaztzis, and A. McKee. 2013. *Primal Leadership: Unleashing the Power of Emotional Intelligence*. Boston: Harvard Business Review Press.

Gunn, C. 2017. "A Lesson in Humility." Ben Franklin Circles (blog). Published April 5. https://benfranklincircles.org/humility/a-lesson-in-humility.

Hixon, J. G., and W. B. Swann. 1993. "When Does Introspection Bear Fruit? Self-Reflection, Self-Insight, and Interpersonal Choices." *Journal of Personality and Social Psychology* 64 (1): 35–43.

Hocutt, M. 1974. "Aristotle's Four Becauses." *Philosophy* 49 (190): 385–99.

Leaf, C. 2013. *Switch On Your Brain: The Key to Peak Happiness, Thinking, and Health*. Grand Rapids, MI: Baker Books.

Magee, J., D. Gruenfeld, D. Keltner, and A. Galinsky. 2005. "Leadership and the Psychology of Power." In *The Psychology of Leadership: New Perspectives and Research*, edited by D. Messick and R. Kramer, 275–94. Mahwah, NJ: Psychology Press.

Mayo Clinic. 2020. "Mindfulness Exercises." Published September 15. www.mayoclinic.org/healthy-lifestyle/consumer-health/ in-depth/mindfulness-exercises/art-20046356.

Miller, K. 2021. "Building Self-Awareness: 16 Activities and Tools for Meaningful Change." PositivePsychology.com. Published May 31. https://positivepsychology.com/ building-self-awareness-activities/.

Patel, D. 2017. "15 Destructive Habits Every Leader Should Let Go Of." *Forbes* Leadership (blog). Published October 9. www. forbes.com/sites/deeppatel/2017/10/09/15-destructive-habits-every-leader-needs-to-let-go-of/.

Samuels, M. 2007. "'Voodoo' Death Revisited: The Modern Lessons of Neurocardiology." *Cleveland Clinic Journal of Medicine* 74 (2 suppl. 1): S8–S16.

Shay, J. 2014. "Moral Injury." *Psychoanalytic Psychology* 31 (2): 182–91.

Taylor, S., D. Kluemper, W. M. Bowler, and J. Halbesleben. 2019. "Why People Get Away with Being Rude at Work." *Harvard Business Review*. Published July 10. https://hbr.org/2019/07/ why-people-get-away-with-being-rude-at-work.

Thompson, R. 1994. "Emotion Regulation: A Theme in Search of Definition." *Monographs of the Society for Research in Child Development* 59 (2–3): 25–52.

Vago, D. R., and D. A. Silbersweig. 2012. "Self-Awareness, Self-Regulation, and Self-Transcendence (S-ART): A Framework for Understanding the Neurobiological Mechanisms of Mindful-ness." *Frontiers in Human Neuroscience*. Published October 25. www.ncbi.nlm.nih.gov/pmc/articles/PMC3480633/.

CHAPTER 3

Self-Management

He who reigns within himself, and rules passions,
desires, and fears, is more than a king.

—John Milton

ALMOST WEEKLY, we can see media reports about leaders in high-level positions of authority and power making catastrophic, career-ending behavior choices.

- The CEO of a group of hospice and home health companies received a 15-year prison sentence for his role in a $150 million healthcare fraud case, involving money laundering and obstruction of justice.
- The owner of two pharmacies and a management company in Florida pleaded guilty to his role in a $931 million healthcare fraud scheme.
- Three spine care providers agreed to pay a total of $1.72 million to resolve allegations that they submitted improper

claims to Medicare for electroacupuncture using a device that does not qualify for reimbursement.

- A former medical researcher received a 30-month prison sentence for conspiring to steal trade secrets concerning the identification and treatment of pediatric medical conditions.

It is highly improbable that any of these people woke up one morning looking for ways to destroy their own lives. It is more likely that these people lacked the skill of self-management. They became so insulated by their inflated sense of self-worth and value that they lost sight of behavioral boundaries related to their thoughts about themselves, their thoughts about others, and their willingness to accept candid feedback to guide their behavior choices. Derailing a career is a gradual process of repeating bad thinking and of creating disruptive emotions that result in highly unproductive behaviors. How can so many bright, intelligent, highly educated, talented people behave so foolishly? Life coach expert Jim Rohn (2007, 101) summarizes it well:

> Failure is not a single, cataclysmic event. We do not fail overnight. Failure is the inevitable result of an accumulation of poor thinking and poor choices. To put it more simply, failure is nothing more than a few errors in judgment repeated every day.
>
> Now, why would someone make an error in judgment and then be so foolish as to repeat it every day? *The answer is because he or she does not think that it matters.* (Italics added.)

Research in business, behavioral science, and organizational development indicates that highly effective leaders have an aptitude for self-management. They have a set of personal core values, they have a personal purpose statement, they understand their behavior preferences, they regulate their thoughts and emotions, and they are keenly aware of the need to create and sustain positive interpersonal relationships. Conversely, the lack of self-management is a primary cause of ineffective leadership, disrupting the performance of teams and corrupting organizational culture.

Sadly, most organizations avoid fixing the biggest hindrance to their success—leaders who are not held accountable for their behavior incompetence. Mission, vision, and values statements adorning the hallways are meaningless if they are contradicted daily by the behaviors of the organization's leaders.

Self-management is an exercise in mental and emotional strength. It is not easy to practice in a chaotic environment, and self-management skills do not develop overnight. Once mastered, however, self-management is a powerful ally against all kinds of personal and professional behavioral challenges. In simple terms, self-management is the key to developing effective leadership and ultimately improving overall quality of life. That is why self-management is the dependent variable of our effective leadership equation.

Effective leadership = $f(x)$(self-awareness) × (self-management)

The more a leader engages in the practice of self-management, the greater the impact of self-awareness, driving leadership effectiveness to higher levels. Whereas self-awareness is the knowing element of the effective leadership equation, self-management is the doing element that makes it all come together. In this sense, self-management is the key to creating leadership effectiveness, employee engagement, and ultimately organizational performance. Without self-management we are unable to lead ourselves with our own upper brain, let alone lead the upper brains of others.

WHEN LEADERS LACK SELF-MANAGEMENT SKILLS

Leaders who display strong self-management skills tend to be more effective and successful in their work. These skills assist leaders in staying attentive to the six science-based leadership performance factors: productivity, quality, initiative, collaboration, problem-solving, and adapting to change. Even if you believe that your self-management skills are deficient, you can use the skills we will provide you to improve them and align your behavior appropriately to these predictable performance factors.

Teams perform to the level of their leader's effectiveness in self-management. Accordingly, there are many consequences to employee engagement and organizational performance when leaders lack self-management skills. Perhaps the costliest and least visible failing for a leader lacking self-management is in what we call *span of control*, or management of complexity. Frequently, people are promoted into higher levels of leadership responsibility based on previous performance, not on an evaluation of their capacity to manage increasing levels of performance responsibilities. These people tend to be successful based on their own technical abilities in limited areas of responsibility and scope of work. When a person moves up the leadership ladder, they gain increased autonomy in defining the specific parameters of their work. To achieve desired performance outcomes with this autonomy requires integration, collaboration, and supportive, multidimensional networks that include a host of professional specialties.

As span of control increases, demands for performance outcomes are more of a challenge for leaders who have not embraced the discipline of self-management. They can no longer achieve on their efforts alone, and they lack the ability to create and develop a high-performing team. The response in these scenarios is for these leaders to get really busy, overschedule their time, and micromanage the work processes of their teams. They are constantly reacting, putting out fires, and handling one crisis after another. Leaders tend to confuse all this activity with real productivity and think, "Everyone is really busy. There is a buzz of activity. Therefore, we must be producing results."

The error is confusing all the activity—how busy everyone is—with actual productivity. This behavior might produce short-term gains but cannot create long-term, sustainable performance. There is a difference between the performance behavior that happens because of good self-management and the performance behavior that happens despite poor self-management. When the behavior of leaders is fragmented, without focus and direction, they lose sight of their teams' priorities. Team members struggle to work for leaders who cannot establish a clear direction with clear work priorities. If a leader does not have self-management skills and is constantly shifting from one priority to another, engagement suffers. As team members are left to figure things out on their own, the increased stress and frustration often lead to conflict, disengagement, burnout, and an overall lack of performance.

The concept of span of control operates on a leadership principle that affects many leaders without their awareness and can derail their careers if they do not learn to pay attention to it. The higher you rise on the leadership ladder, the more strategic your work becomes. Your daily duties and methods of completing them are no longer clearly defined. You gain the freedom to chart your own course and your own performance outcomes. This increased freedom comes with the additional responsibility to self-manage your focus, your energy, and the direction of your work. Emerging leaders get specific instructions on the execution of processes and practices to produce results. It is a senior leader's prerogative to create those processes and practices; senior leaders are in control of *how* the organization achieves the desired outcomes.

In all the hustle and bustle, leaders can easily neglect self-management. Another leadership principle is that no one else can self-manage you. Self-management is a personal requirement. Other people can assist you with aspects of self-management, but ultimately you must choose to do it for yourself. In the long run, engaging in the practice of self-management serves your own legitimate self-interests, the interests of your team members, and the overall interests of the organization.

DEVELOPING SELF-MANAGEMENT

Just as self-awareness includes both inner and external awareness, we divide self-management competency into two skill sets as well: inner (personal) self-management and external (relational) self-management. To help you see this concept clearly, think about professional athletes who speak in terms of their inner game and their outer game. Consider personal self-management your inner game and relational self-management your external game (Nevins 2020).

Much of the contemporary work on self-management appropriately focuses on the external game of relational self-management. As we have already discussed, in an operating environment of increasing complexity and change, leaders must have the behavior skills required to calm the disruptive elements of their team members' lower brains. Additionally, these same behavior skills are necessary to help team members regulate their thoughts and emotions so they can connect to and ignite their upper brains for performance. These external self-management skills promote connection, collaboration, and engagement to drive performance outcomes.

The other half of this self-management skill, the half that gets less attention, is the inner game of self-management. How well are you leading yourself with your own upper brain? What are you doing to calm your own thoughts and emotions so you are controlling the disruption of your own lower brain in times of stress, frustration, and conflict?

The primary function of effective leadership is to create a compelling vision, move people toward a common objective, and provide collective well-being for the members of the organization. Without mastery of inner self-management skills to ground you and guide you, you will lose the impact of your external self-management on your effective leadership of others. We take a balanced approach teaching the key elements of inner and external self-management, providing leaders the greatest opportunity to lead themselves and others effectively from the upper brain.

DETERMINING YOUR INNER SELF-MANAGEMENT

We offer three primary development skills to help develop and navigate your inner self-management effectively. Employing a sailing metaphor, successful navigation requires that a ship have a rudder, a helm, and a navigator. The rudder is essential to managing the direction of a ship, particularly to changing directions. The helm, historically, was a tiller or wheel used for steering the ship. Finally, the navigator physically controls the movements of the helm, sending instructions to the rudder and guiding the overall movement of the ship. These three components must work in harmony to complete a successful journey through waters full of volatility, uncertainty, complexity, and ambiguity.

Navigating the emotional terrain of the human brain (fear, loss, doubt, and anxiety) requires the harmonious cooperation of personal core values (a rudder), a personal purpose statement (a helm), and a commitment to personal accountability and responsibility (a navigator). Until you learn to manage the disruptive elements of your inner self, you will be challenged to manage the disruptive elements of your external self as you navigate the perils of your business environment.

Personal Core Values

The first step to inner self-management is to develop and sustain a resilient and reliable inner core. The behavior we desire to see in others in our pursuit of performance excellence begins with ourselves. If you do not take this first step, your leadership behavior will be inconsistent and will negatively affect your leadership effectiveness.

The inner core of a person consists of cause-and-effect relationships in the brain between what a person thinks, what that person chooses to believe, and how the brain chemically responds to these thoughts and beliefs to create behavior choices (the cognitive triangle). You are free to make choices about how you focus your attention, and this affects how the chemicals and proteins and wiring of your brain change and function. Scientists are proving every day that the relationship between what you think and how you understand yourself—your core values, thoughts, beliefs, hopes, and desires—has a huge effect on how your brain physically functions (Leaf 2013).

Our core values represent our judgments about what we deem significant. They represent our highest priorities, our most deeply held beliefs, and the fundamental driving forces behind our behavior. Your leadership behavior is a direct reflection of your core values. We cannot observe a value, but we can observe how a person manifests that value with behavior. In the classic book *As a Man Thinketh*, James Allen (1951, 1) wrote these profound words decades before the advent of neuropsychology:

> Man is made and unmade by himself; in the armory of thoughts he forges the weapons which will destroy him. He also fashions the tools with which he builds for himself heavenly mansions of joy and strength and peace. By the right choice and true application of thought, man ascends to Divine Perfection. . . . Between these two extremes are all the grades of character and man is their maker and their master.

We always know what a person really believes by observing how that person behaves. For example, our personal core values are integrity, compassion, and excellence. Each of these core values translates into observable and measurable behaviors. You can recognize when a person is behaving with integrity; they exhibit truthful behavior, their behavior is reliable, and they follow the rules. Likewise, a person with the core value of compassion would reveal that through acts of kindness and gestures of sympathy, and their behavior would be empathic and caring toward others. Finally, someone who values excellence would demonstrate a high regard for quality, precision, and accuracy, adhering to published standards of performance and seeking continuous improvement.

The stability of your inner core—your system of thoughts and beliefs—is the source of your performance behavior, which directly affects your level of leadership effectiveness and performance. A corrupt core will lead to ineffective, disruptive, and unproductive behavior. An ethical core, on the other hand, will lead to productive, collaborative behavior that drives influence, effectiveness, and peak performance.

There is great power in knowing your inner self. As a rational being, you have the capacity to create and control your own thoughts and make your own choices. You have the power to transform your inner core and shape your destiny. Do not forget this simple truth: The outer conditions of your life will always be in harmony with your inner core.

You actively choose your beliefs and values and build your life on that foundation. You live and work in a way that is consistent with who you are on the inside. You develop willpower as your core beliefs become stronger than your impulses. As a result, you live a life of integrity and earn the trust and respect of others. When you achieve this level of self-management, you can create and sustain a team that is able to overcome immense challenges and accomplish great things of lasting value.

Personal Purpose Statement

Effective leadership behavior is about making a difference in the lives of other people and your organization. The first step in this transformational journey is identifying your inner core and then living consistently from that core in your daily behavior. One thing that maintains alignment between our inner core and our outer behavior is a constant focus and connection to personal purpose.

Your *purpose statement* is a reflection of who you are and what you bring to the world—starting today. By crafting a personal purpose statement, you can powerfully communicate your intentions and motivate your team to share an attractive and inspiring common vision of the future. Your personal purpose statement defines your existence, giving meaning and value to your life, so you can engage in activities that will change the world for good. In the words of paralympian Amy Purdy, "When we embrace the things that make us unique, our true and remarkable capabilities are revealed" (Connor 2014).

Do you have a personal purpose statement? Do you have a clear focus? Have you allowed yourself to lose your passion, your dreams, and your zeal for excellence? Have you allowed yourself to see the work you do merely as a job and a paycheck, going through daily routines and motions, lacking a sense of purpose and vision? Are you settling for less than your best? In writing a personal purpose statement, you will discover your true and remarkable capabilities, which you will use throughout the exciting journey before you.

You do not need to settle for second best in your life or in your work. A personal purpose statement clarifies your personal beliefs and values about what success and achievement means to you. Your personal purpose statement defines what you want to achieve in work and in life and expresses it in measurable goals and objectives. Having this clarity of purpose also makes it easier to change unproductive behaviors that are keeping you from achieving what you truly desire. If you cannot identify the things that matter most to you in life, you will not be able to cherish and protect them.

Pause and reflect about where you are in life at this moment. Create a list of the ten best things you have achieved at this point in your life. Perhaps you scored highly on a professional board exam, played a key role on an important team, produced the best sales figures in a period, did something that made a key difference in someone else's life, or delivered a project that meant a lot for your business. Start a victory journal listing these accomplishments in a smartly formatted journal or in your favorite note-taking application. The key is to put these victories somewhere you can get to them quickly. Then spend a few minutes each week reading over this list of accomplishments, enjoying the success you have already experienced. This exercise will help you maintain a positive focus, reconnect to your core values, and live your personal purpose statement in your daily life choices.

Everyone wants to succeed and to achieve something of meaning and value in their lives. Those people who consistently succeed are ordinary people who are relentless in living their lives according to their purpose statements. As a result, they have extraordinary levels of focus, discipline, and passion linked to their purpose and vision.

- *Focus* is the ability to filter out distractions and direct your full attention to accomplishing a mission or fulfilling a dream. *It is fixed attention.*
- *Discipline* is the ability to stay focused on what needs to be done until your mission or dream is accomplished. Discipline is the consistent doing of an action despite the fact that it is sometimes uncomfortable, inconvenient, or difficult. *It is dedicated action.*
- *Passion* is the ability to stay motivated, emotionally engaged, and tenaciously persistent in the pursuit of your mission. *It is intense emotion.*

What it takes to be an effective leader is no secret. The literature is full of articles with a wide variety of traits attributed to effective leaders. You need to remember, however, that effective leadership is more than a list of traits. The key is manifesting these traits in daily behaviors. Demonstrating these traits in your behavior requires training and coaching in how to move these traits from the inner world of self to the external world of others.

Whatever your current circumstances, you will rise or fall, succeed or fail, by your ability to manage your thoughts and attitudes, because they frame your purpose and vision. When you discover purpose for your life, you will also discover the conviction to live with sincerity and the will to pursue the things that matter most in becoming a difference maker for yourself and for others.

Personal Accountability and Responsibility

In every situation, highly effective leaders take full responsibility for the quality of the results and the overall performance of their teams and organizations. Taking responsibility means being accountable for your choices and recognizing that your attitude and actions make a huge impact on the performance behavior of others. In the words of Dr. Henry Cloud (2013, 28), "Leaders are ridiculously in charge. In the end, as a leader, you are always going to get what you create or what you allow."

Effective leaders demonstrate vital strengths to achieve their performance objectives: the drive to achieve results, the ability to accept personal responsibility for those results, the willingness to take ownership of self (thoughts, emotions, attitudes, and behaviors), the capacity to cultivate collaboration and team building, and finally, the ability to establish and maintain highly effective relationships.

Taking ownership of self means being aware of and choosing effective responses to the circumstances and challenges you face daily. People who accept responsibility and take ownership of self do not shift blame for poor results and outcomes to others. They do not procrastinate; rather, they take action efficiently and effectively. They never make excuses and play the role of victim in difficult situations. Instead, effective leaders approach life and work asking, What can I do to make a difference? How can I contribute to a better outcome? What do I need to do to get better?

Note that taking responsibility goes beyond merely accepting blame. An effective leader who is asking *what* and *how* is moving toward resolving problems, creating opportunities, and managing events with a positive response to create optimal outcomes out of bad situations. While accepting personal accountability and responsibility is a vital aspect of effective leadership, far too many leaders overlook the fact that they are "ridiculously in charge."

How we choose to see a problem is always the real problem. How we choose to see something, our perspective and perception, is greatly influenced by our life experiences. We need to understand that we do not always see things in their complete context or with unbiased objectivity.

Responsibility and accountability function as the levers that activate thoughtful, effective action. When you take responsibility, you improve your quality of life and work, you improve your behavior pattern, and you commit to continuous learning and growth. The result is a life lived to your full potential. It is unrealistic—even a bit foolish—to think you can improve your life and work if are you unwilling to take responsibility for your attitudes and actions.

Life is about choices. We mistakenly think that life is about events. The important thing to remember is that we are not defined by events. What defines who we are is how we choose to respond to these events. Really important life events are lived at the point of the spear—defining moments of truth, as some performance professionals say. You find yourself in a circumstance to which you must respond without the help of others. Hence, the choices you make in the moment, during those events, define the direction of your life.

Change and chaos are constant in our rapid-paced, knowledge- and technology-driven culture. Another constant is at play in this culture, as well; namely, how human beings tend to respond to this change and chaos, and the stress that accompanies both of them. Before any real behavioral change can take place in our lives, we must be convinced that change is real, possible, and holds the promise of improved outcomes.

Change is inevitable and so, it would seem, is our resistance to it. Yet, in the midst of this change and chaos, effective leaders and their organizations continue to thrive, to grow, and to sustain a high level of performance excellence.

The best leadership skills begin with the way people choose to think and the way the brain functions at optimal levels. Our brains, as we will discover in the next chapter, are designed to work in specific ways, with specific functions, to produce predictable outcomes.

Here are five strategies to assist you in creating a mindset of accepting personal accountability and responsibility:

1. Just as companies are rightfully concerned about how they are viewed by customers or shareholders, consider taking time to reflect on how your behavior is experienced by your personal stakeholders—your direct reports, your peers, and your clients. Go through a formal 360° leadership assessment process, or simply find a leadership assessment form and use it to reflect on how others in your team would rate you on each performance dimension.

2. At the end of each day, take a few minutes to mentally review your day. Think about significant conversations you had, meetings you attended, emails you sent, and other actions you undertook. Are you satisfied with your performance? Could you have done better? This exercise will inspire you to plan your next day around your highest purpose. Getting into this habit of daily introspection will pay dividends in the long run. Finally, find one or two key team members and ask them to respond to this question: "On a scale of one to ten, how effective was I as your leader/team member today?" If you get any answer other than a ten, ask them to tell you one thing you could have done differently to rate a ten. This simple accountability tool will do wonders for building your influence with others.

3. Decide to hold yourself accountable for developing other leaders. By mentoring a protégé, you strengthen your own leadership skills and reinforce your determination to be self-accountable as you become their role model.

4. When something goes wrong, look inwardly for solutions. Remember, the difficult events challenge our response and our self-accountability. Martin Luther King Jr. ([1963] 1981, 26) said, "The ultimate measure of a man is not where he stands in moments of comfort and convenience, but where he stands at times of challenge and controversy."

5. In the words often attributed to Molière, a seventeenth-century French dramatist, "It is not only what we do, but also what we do not do, for which we are accountable." Is there anything that you are avoiding doing that needs to be done? For example, are you putting off a difficult conversation? Do you owe someone a sincere apology? Are you delaying any important decisions? Are you delegating responsibilities that should stay in your court?

Our habits are part of a cause-and-effect relationship between what we believe to be true about the world around us and the coinciding mental models and patterns our brains create to align with those beliefs. Habit change is hard because our brains prefer the path of least resistance. To create new neuronal connections, your brain needs you to convince it that you really want to change. Taking responsibility and ownership of self requires a constant reexamination of these neuronal connections to ensure you are behaving with the most effective mental models possible for high performance outcomes.

DETERMINING YOUR EXTERNAL SELF-MANAGEMENT

There is immense pressure in every industry today for leaders to produce results. Leaders are working longer and harder to generate new revenue streams to sustain and grow financial margins.

Consequently, for today's leaders, understanding the impact of behavior on the performance capacity of colleagues and team members is an indispensable skill for creating high-performing teams and driving performance outcomes. There are ways that leaders can behave that make vision and strategy work. There are also ways that leaders can behave that make it impossible for the brains of their team members to execute that vision and strategy to get results.

In the proper conditions, the human brain has a marvelous capacity for growth, achievement, and performance. In the proper conditions, people can think, behave, and connect with their roles at a high level of engagement and at the full potential of their performance capacity. When leaders have the skills to create these conditions and function as the guardian of these conditions, their people can produce results at consistently high levels. This process is what we call leading the brains of your people to higher levels of performance. When leaders fail to create these performance conditions, they disturb the performance brains of their people. As a leader, you disturb the performance brains of your people at your own performance peril.

We offer a primary development skill to help cultivate and direct your external self-management skills effectively. The research identifies this skill as *focused attention*. When leaders learn and apply focused attention, they position themselves to exhibit their own performance behavior in ways that maximize both their executive presence and their leadership presence with their teams. Leaders cannot create teams that display healthy performance behaviors and drive results unless they are capable of modeling those behaviors for them.

Focused Attention

Neuroscientists are discovering brain centers for just about everything. We have focused on two of those brain centers already—the upper brain, built for performance and achievement, and the lower brain, built for survival. Part of the problem with living in the twenty-first century is that, with a brain center for just about everything, we *want* just about everything. Our ability to focus and manage the demands we are putting on our brains is deteriorating.

Hougaard and Carter (2018) found that 73 percent of leaders feel distracted from their current task either "some" or "most" of the time, and that 67 percent of leaders view their minds as cluttered, with multiple, raging thoughts, and no clear prioritization of the tasks that matter most to their performance outcomes. This lack of focused attention is wreaking havoc on our ability to get things done.

This phenomenon of doing more and achieving less led the authors of *The Attention Economy* to write, "Understanding and managing attention is now the single most important determinant of business success" (Davenport and Beck 2001, 3). That statement was published more than twenty years ago. Things have only gotten worse since then.

In a seminar at a national leadership congress for healthcare leaders, we were teaching concepts related to leadership effectiveness and creating high-performing teams. This topic of focused attention became part of a heated conversation during the question-and-answer period, with one CEO protesting the "unrealistic expectation" we had created for senior leaders being able to set appropriate boundaries on their time, tasks, and effectiveness. We really connected with this leader's emotional distress while describing a standard workday: 12 to 14 hours long, back-to-back meetings, one crisis after another.

The emotional trigger for this leader was our suggestion that leaders should stop sending emails to their team members at 10 o'clock at night and on weekends. The CEO protested that the only time they could ever get to their email was after hours or on the weekends. Here was the caveat, "Even though I send them late at night and on the weekends, I have told my team members not to read or answer them until the following workday." Knowing human nature as you do, if you worked for this CEO, how likely is it that you would ignore emails until the following workday? What if a colleague answered them and you waited? Would this leader consider you less energetic, think of you as displaying less initiative, judge you as lacking a high level of motivation and engagement?

To help this CEO understand how leader behavior affects team member performance, we conducted an ad hoc poll of all seminar participants working below the C-suite level: "How many of you would answer after-hours and weekend emails even if your senior leader had told you not to do it?" Without exception, they all agreed that they would answer the emails. A younger and sympathetic emerging leader offered this CEO some help on this problem by asking if they knew how to use a delayed send option in email. Specifically, the comment was, "You can write your emails late at night but then they do not have be delivered until the following morning." At that suggestion, the CEO bristled overtly and stormed out of the meeting room.

The science is clear and indisputable—the external management skill of focused attention as a performance behavior is what makes a leader truly exceptional. The good news is that with even the smallest incremental changes, over time you can learn to regain and maintain your focus. From a neurological perspective it is not easy, because we have brain centers that are constantly scanning our surroundings and gathering new data inputs that require our attention (Pickersgill, Martin, and Cunningham-Burley 2015). Many of these brain centers ensured human survival in ancient times. Focus occurs in our upper brain—the prefrontal cortex. Distraction and constant scanning of sensory input comes from the lower brain's limbic system—the amygdala and the posterior cingulate cortex, to be exact.

This neurophysiological polarity—the tension between the upper and lower brain—is why focus training needs to be a part of every leadership development program as a means of creating external self-management proficiency. When we are able to lead ourselves and others from the upper brain, we can quiet irrelevant noise, focus in the moment on the task at hand, engage our team members in meaningful ways, and increase our leadership effectiveness.

Based on our research and fieldwork with senior leaders, five strategies are particularly effective in creating focused attention. We adapted the following list from "The R Factor," a leadership training program by Tim Kight, and from Mind Tools, a career development website founded by James Manktelow and Rachel Thompson.

1. *Manage your goals.* Make the *decision* to achieve. Get focused. Define success for yourself. Decide what you want to accomplish in life and at work and make it your purpose. If you aim at nothing, you will hit it. Identify, pursue, and achieve your goals!

2. *Manage your action.* Create the *discipline* to achieve. The best results are produced by those who take the most effective action. Set goals, then develop and implement an action plan for achieving them. Your plan focuses attention on the specific, daily actions you need to take to achieve your goals and fulfill your mission. Sustained action over time produces results.

3. *Manage your attitude.* Ignite the *passion* to achieve. Your attitude is not something that happens to you. You are the architect of your frame of mind. You determine whether your mindset is positive or negative. You choose your attitude! As William James said, "The greatest discovery of my generation is that a human being can alter his life by altering his attitudes of mind." Your attitude sets the mood for everyone around you.

4. *Manage change.* Develop the *flexibility* to achieve. Success requires constant adjustment. It is your responsibility to make the change you need to achieve your goals. If what you are doing is not working, then change it. Doing

more of what doesn't work, doesn't work. Success and achievement belong to people who are able to manage change and adapt to new circumstances.

5. *Manage adversity.* Cultivate the *mental toughness* to achieve. Adversity is an inevitable part of life. No one wants it, but everyone experiences it. Managing adversity requires you to develop a great deal of optimism. Optimists view adversity in their lives as temporary, specific, and external (i.e., not entirely their fault). Their optimist mindset informs their emotions; life is not about what is happening to you but how you choose to respond to what is happening to you.

All the suggestions and strategies we have included for you in this discussion of self-management will develop and strengthen your leadership behavior—if you do them. Knowing your inner core, staying connected to your purpose, accepting personal accountability, and maintaining laser-like, focused attention on the things that matter most will benefit you greatly as you navigate a world of constant change, chaos, and uncertainty.

KEY TAKEAWAYS

- Research in business, behavioral science, and organizational development indicates that highly effective leaders have an aptitude for self-management.
- The more a leader engages in the practice of self-management, the greater the impact of self-awareness, driving leadership effectiveness to higher levels.
- Team members struggle to work for leaders who cannot establish a clear direction with clear work priorities.
- The primary function of effective leadership is to create a compelling vision, move people toward a common

objective, and provide collective well-being for the members of the organization.

- As a rational being, you have the capacity to create and control your own thoughts and make your own choices, influencing your destiny.

- Your personal purpose statement defines your existence and gives meaning and value to your life, so you can engage in activities that will change the world for good.

- If you cannot identify the things that matter most to you in life, you will not be able to cherish and protect them.

- When you discover purpose for your life, you will also discover the conviction to live with sincerity and the will to pursue the things that matter most.

- When we are able to lead ourselves and others from the upper brain, we can quiet irrelevant noise, focus in the moment on the task at hand, engage our team members in meaningful ways, and increase our leadership effectiveness.

PUT IT TO WORK

1. Identify and discuss your personal core values and the core values of your organization with trusted colleagues and team members. Ask yourselves the following questions:
    - Why are these values important?
    - What core values do you share with the organization?
    - How do your personal core values align with your daily personal behavior and the behaviors of the organization?

2. Using the values exercise available from Carnegie Mellon University's Career and Professional Development Center (www.cmu.edu/career/resource-library/career-exploration/my-career-path.html, at "mySelf") craft your own set of

personal core values. If you have previously done a values exercise, do it again and see whether your values have shifted or you have added any new ones. Try to limit the number of core values to guide your life to three primary core values.

3. Ask yourself a few questions about your list of course values to determine how you acquired these values:
   - Why is each of these values important to me?
   - Why do I want these values to be part of my inner core, given all the other values I could have chosen?

4. Create your personal purpose statement. Whatever your current circumstances, you will rise or fall, succeed or fail, by your ability to manage your thoughts and attitude, because they frame your mission and vision. (This guide will help you complete your personal purpose statement: www.linkedin.com/pulse/20140609202917-14809800-how-to-write-a-personal-purpose-statement/.)

5. Without conviction, leaders rarely accomplish anything of lasting value—things that really make a significant difference. What do you believe to be true with great passion and conviction? Have you ever made a list of things you believe strongly and then identified why you feel so passionately about those things? Take a few minutes to answer this question.

6. Use *Harvard Business Review*'s "Mindfulness Assessment" (https://hbr.org/2017/03/assessment-how-mindful-are-you) to assess your current ability to maintain focus and awareness.

7. Look at your schedule and block time to evaluate where you can hit pause for five to ten minutes, three or four times a day. Use this time for the following self-management activities:
   - Make journal entries about how your day is progressing, emotions you are currently experiencing,

and elements of distraction that have popped up as you are moving through your daily schedule.

- Reframe and refocus your perspective. If you are thinking about an earlier meeting or personal encounter in a negative way, what could you do to think differently and flip the negative to a positive?

- Hit reset on your self-management focus. Use deep breathing exercises to calm yourself, reconnect to your upper brain, and find a way to express gratitude and thankfulness for something wonderful in your life.

REFERENCES

Allen, J. 1951. *As a Man Thinketh*. Mount Vernon, NY: Peter Pauper Press.

Cloud, H. 2013. *Boundaries for Leaders: Results, Relationships, and Being Ridiculously in Charge*. New York: Harper Collins.

Connor, J. 2014. "How to Write a Personal Purpose Statement." LinkedIn (blog). Published June 9. www.linkedin.com/pulse/20140609202917-14809800-how-to-write-a-personal-purpose-statement/.

Davenport, T., and J. Beck. 2001. *The Attention Economy: Understanding the New Currency of Business*. Boston: Harvard Business School Press.

Hougaard, R., and J. Carter. 2018. *The Mind of the Leader: How to Lead Yourself, Your People, and Your Organization for Extraordinary Results*. Boston: Harvard Business School Publishing.

King, M. L., Jr. (1963) 1981. *Strength to Love*. Boston: Beacon Press.

Leaf, C. 2013. *Switch On Your Brain: The Key to Peak Happiness, Thinking, and Health*. Grand Rapids, MI: Baker Publishing Group.

Nevins, M. 2020. "To Lead 'Out There,' Start 'In Here': The Inner Game of Leadership." *Forbes* (blog). Published December 2. www.forbes.com/sites/hillennevins/2020/12/02/to-lead-out-there-start-in-here--the-inner-game-of-leadership/.

Pickersgill, M., P. Martin, and S. Cunningham-Burley. 2015. "The Changing Brain: Neuroscience and the Enduring Import of Everyday Experience." *Public Understanding of Science* 24 (7): 878–92.

Rohn, J. 2007. "The Formula for Failure and Success." In *The Power of Coaching: Engaging Excellence in Others!*, by M. MacDonald, 100–105. Grass Valley, CA: PLI Publishing.

PART II

Engagement

When people are financially invested, they want a return. When people are emotionally invested, they want to contribute.

—Simon Sinek

A SENIOR LEADER of a hospital system struggling with employee satisfaction contracted with us to help them turn things around with their team members. The key objective of our performance behavior project was to help the members of the organization connect to their work and improve relationships within their teams, in turn improving patient safety, quality of care, and the patient experience. Our first challenge was getting the organization's senior leadership to understand that there is a huge difference between employee satisfaction and employee engagement.

Employee satisfaction describes the key aspects of a worker enjoying their job—but not necessarily doing the job well at a high level of performance outcomes. A person can have a high degree of satisfaction regardless of the behavior effectiveness of their leader. A satisfied employee has no problem coming to work and doing as little as necessary to collect a paycheck and go home. Imagine the employee who gets to show up to work late and leave early without contributing anything to the key objectives and strategy of the organization.

Engaged employees, on the other hand, are committed to helping their company achieve all its goals. Engaged employees are motivated to show up to work every day and do everything in their power to help their company succeed. Effective leadership is necessary to achieve employee engagement. Employee engagement and leadership effectiveness are inextricably connected, and not just in terms of employee satisfaction.

According to the "Employee Job Satisfaction and Engagement" report from the Society for Human Resource Management (2016), US workers were more satisfied with their jobs in 2016 than they had been in the previous ten years. At least 88 percent of employees were at least somewhat satisfied, while 37 percent were very satisfied. The survey findings indicated the top three factors driving job satisfaction were respectful treatment (67%), compensation/pay (63%), and benefits (60%).

While job satisfaction appeared to be at an all-time high at the time of this study, the same research indicated that employees were only moderately engaged. On a scale of 1 (low engagement) to 5 (high engagement), the average engagement score was 3.8. The top three conditions for engagement were relationships with coworkers (77%), opportunities to use skills and abilities (77%), and meaningfulness of the job (76%). Recall that our objective was to help team members to improve their working relationships and connect their work to organizational objectives. Our client organization's senior leadership had not prioritized leadership behaviors that influence factors such as these—leadership behaviors that could raise employee engagement.

Our second, and most significant, challenge in helping that struggling hospital system was working with a group of 150 mid-tier leaders who had absolutely no desire to work with another consultant on the problem of employee satisfaction. In our first meeting with these leaders, we wanted to demonstrate our commitment to helping them discover and raise their own levels of meaning and value in their work. We asked them to tell us why they thought their teams struggled to get the results that senior leaders desired. As we concluded the meeting, we held a question-and-answer session so the attendees could understand our role and the purpose of the project.

There was a period of silence, and then a voice from the back of the room shouted out, "So what are you going to try and change about us?" Knowing our answer would be critical to the overall success of this engagement project, we said, "Our primary objective is to help all of you, as leaders, create such a wonderful place for everyone to work that you all wake up in the middle of the night disappointed that it is not time to go to work yet!" There was another period of silence and then the same voice shouted out, "Have you passed a drug test lately?" We all laughed. The exchange created a positive emotional connection with everyone in the room, and at the end of our first year into this change initiative, the key performance indicators for this project were at national benchmark standards or higher—including employee engagement. When your team members spend their productive efforts surviving at work rather than thriving at work, performance suffers.

In part I, we established the foundation for performance by looking at the two key elements of leadership effectiveness: self-awareness and self-management. Without effective leadership, it is virtually impossible to obtain high levels of performance outcomes over sustained periods of time. Likewise, we will discover in part II that high levels of performance outcomes are not sustainable without a high degree of organizational engagement. We define the output of engagement as a function of organizational culture and the application of effective leadership behavior:

$$\textbf{Engagement} = \textit{f(x)} \textbf{ (culture)} \times \textbf{(effective leadership)}$$

We also want to emphasize that engagement has two facets: leadership engagement and employee engagement.

Lower levels of effective leadership behaviors degrade the key components of a positive and supportive organizational culture. The result is a lower level of engagement within the organization. Effective leadership requires leaders to understand both performance technical skills and performance behavior skills. A high level of engagement requires leaders to be effective in the doing of performance behaviors, not merely knowing about them. Leaders must be able to leverage effective leadership behaviors to drive the culture of the organization in such a way that leadership effectiveness and culture combine to produce a high level of engagement.

A principle of effective leadership is that you can care about people without leading them, but you can never lead people effectively without caring about them. The leadership competency of performance behavior skills, especially a basic understanding of people—what they think, what they feel, and their legitimate human needs—is very difficult for some leaders to develop. Consequently, the next three chapters will explore the nature of organizational culture and the application of effective leadership behaviors to create and sustain high levels of organizational engagement.

Chapter 4, "The Engagement Equation," will describe the key elements of engagement, explain how to create a high-performing team, and discuss the key blocking behaviors that prevent high engagement. Leaders and their organizations derive many benefits from a highly engaged and committed workforce. Yet many leaders still fail to understand the importance of engagement and lack the desire to create this kind of engagement as a key component of their organizational cultures. A critical factor for creating engagement is understanding how the human brain balances performance on one hand and managing threat dynamics on the other. Personal survival is a legitimate self-interest. Provoke the lower brain—force people to come to work focused on survival—and you destroy any chance of creating an engaged and committed workforce.

Chapter 5, "Creating a Culture of Purpose and Performance," takes you a step further, identifying the key behaviors of a performance culture by emphasizing the need to focus on employees' individual growth and development. We define *culture* as the collection of beliefs, attitudes, and behaviors manifested by a shared social group or organization. To create a culture that focuses on the well-being of people as well as performance, organizational leaders should ensure that the culture includes the social awareness and social management dimensions we outlined in part I. This requires that leaders have a feedback mechanism in place to identify toxic behaviors and enact accountability practices for those behaviors. When leaders lack the ability and will to hold deviant members of their organizations accountable for unacceptable behaviors, they contribute to the disintegration of engagement and performance outcomes.

Chapter 6, "Leadership Behaviors That Drive Engagement," explains how you lead the brains of your people to higher levels of performance. Here you will learn the life-changing distinctions between upper- and lower-brain performance physiology. When you have a performance system that clearly defines roles, goals, and expectations and aligns employees' work to your objectives and key results, and when you conduct regular coaching sessions with the people doing the work of the organization, you will drive performance to higher levels.

There are direct cause-and-effect relationships between effective leadership behaviors, personal well-being, and performance outcomes. These relationships are the result of physiological connections in the brain related to a specific set of neuronal pathways and neurochemicals. By leveraging our understanding of how the human brain responds to external stimuli, positively or negatively, we can drive technical skills, talent, and intellect to the highest levels of performance. This allows us to create organizational cultures where people can grow and flourish while producing results that leaders desire.

Engaged employees love their jobs. They seek continuous personal performance improvement. They are constantly looking for ways to improve themselves and the performance of their organizations. Engaged employees are always waiting on an effective leader to guide them to performance excellence. You can be that kind of effective leader.

KEY TAKEAWAYS

- There is a huge difference between employee satisfaction and employee engagement.
- Employee engagement is the engine that drives organizational performance, and leadership effectiveness is the fuel that powers the engine of engagement.
- You can care about people without leading them, but you can never lead people effectively without caring about them.

REFERENCE

Society for Human Resource Management. 2016. *Employee Job Satisfaction and Engagement: Executive Summary*. Accessed August 31, 2021. www.shrm.org/hr-today/trends-and-forecasting/research-and-surveys/Documents/2016-Employee-Job-Satisfaction-and-Engagement-Report-Executive-Summary.pdf.

CHAPTER 4

The Engagement Equation

There are only three measurements that tell you nearly everything you need to know about your organization's overall performance: employee engagement, customer satisfaction, and cash flow. It goes without saying that no company, small or large, can win over the long run without energized employees who believe in the mission and understand how to achieve it.

—Jack Welch, former CEO of GE

THERE ARE TIMELESS principles that endure from one generation to another. When we neglect these principles, they have a way of drawing our attention.

In 2003, Bill George wrote *Authentic Leadership* to persuade current and future leaders that there was a better way of leading organizations than merely focusing on financial returns. George took a great deal of time to examine the relationships between leaders and the people they lead. The engagement equation that arose from his work is one timeless principle that is worth sharing with you as a present-day leader.

Great teams make for great organizations. Those great teams do not happen by accident; they are created and cultivated by the positive emotional connections that the people on those teams share with an effective leader. The foundation on which effective leaders build these relationships is itself built on the central proposition of shared purpose and values. The neurochemical cocktail in our brains converts this proposition of shared purpose and values into performance engagement behaviors that generate superior business outcomes.

Superior results do not happen without an engaged workforce. An engaged workforce does not happen without effective leadership. It is simple neuroscience that the human brain works from achievement drivers on the one hand and survival drivers on the other.

We will discuss a formal definition of employee engagement momentarily. First, we want to look at the key components of the second of our three evidenced-based equations that comprise our integrated and systematic approach for leadership development and performance management:

$$\text{Engagement} = f(x) \text{ (culture)} \times \text{(effective leadership)}$$

Leaders and their organizations derive a significant number of benefits from a highly engaged and committed workforce. Yet many leaders still fail to understand the importance of engagement and lack the desire to create this kind of engagement as a key component of their organizational cultures. To create engagement, leaders must understand how the human brain functions for performance on one hand and manages threat dynamics on the other.

As a simple metaphor, effective leaders are neurochemical bartenders, mixing neurochemical cocktails in the brains of their people through every personal encounter and in every team meeting. As a leader, your behavior can affect people by producing positive or negative emotional triggers (Goleman, Boyaztzis, and McKee 2013). These triggers then send signals to various parts of people's brains, greatly affecting how they choose to respond to you. A cluster of brain cells called *mirror neurons* is responsible for these responsive behaviors, and mirror neurons have a collective influence in a group of people. For example, when a leader criticizes a team member publicly, we all feel the sting of that rebuke. The resulting mirror neuron activity tells us, "I am not safe," and consequently, engagement and performance suffer.

In any human relationship and social network, there is a constant interplay, a mental dance of neurons (brain cells) creating an assortment of neurochemical cocktails. Everyone gets to bring their own mixers to this party, but the leader controls the main ingredients of the drinks. Everyone takes their mental cues from the leader's behavior. An approachable leader creates a team atmosphere that encourages mutual exchange of information, ideas, and opinions; a moody leader creates an atmosphere of fear, loss, and doubt. Is it any wonder that the performance of teams with effective leaders is higher than that of teams with ineffective leaders?

Your team members' levels of engagement and performance depend on your behavior. Your behavior is either lighting up their upper brains for performance or blowing up their brains by triggering a fight or flight response. When you lead with the understanding that you are a neurochemical bartender, you become more aware of how your behavior provokes emotional responses in your team members. If you remain positive and hopeful in difficult times, then they will tend to follow your lead and remain positive and hopeful too.

Creating and cultivating engagement in your team requires you to understand the neuroscience of functional social networks, and modern organizations are nothing if not a collection of social networks. As a leader, you choose whether to foster meaning, value, and purpose in your team's and organization's social networks. You can, through your own behavior, nurture positive connections with members of your team to create and cultivate engagement and drive performance. You can also choose to ignore this principle—at your own performance peril. This is a timeless principle, worth learning and practicing; and the best time to learn it and practice it is now.

DEFINING EMPLOYEE ENGAGEMENT

The level of employee engagement in your teams is a direct reflection of the effectiveness of your leadership and your organization's culture, as observed by measurable results. Again, these are science-based cause-and-effect relationships.

To gain a clear understanding of what employee engagement is, we should first discuss what it is not:

- Employee engagement is not satisfaction. Satisfaction is about someone liking their job. Engagement is someone doing their job well to advance the interests and objectives of the organization.
- Employee engagement is not about making people happy. It is about providing people the opportunity to discover meaning, value, and purpose in their work.
- Employee engagement is not about motivation. Even if it were about motivation, however, the research of Chip Heath at Stanford University clearly indicates that leaders lack the ability to judge what motivates employees (Morse 2003). As Peter Drucker supposedly said, "We know nothing about motivation. We just write books about it."
- Employee engagement is not about empowerment, but engagement and empowerment are related; empowerment provides the structure and the means for employee engagement to flourish.

So, knowing what engagement is not, what is the meaning of *engagement*? Gallup (2021), which has studied engagement for decades, defines engaged employees as "those who are involved in, enthusiastic about, and committed to their work and workplace." People who are engaged show up to work hoping to advance the causes, objectives, goals, and purpose of the organization. By observing and measuring engagement behaviors, leaders can gain perspective on the effectiveness of organizational culture. Following are some of the key elements of engagement:

- Employee engagement is first and foremost an emotional commitment to the organization and its goals.
- Employee engagement is a state and a behavior that makes employees feel passionate about their work.
- Engaged employees care about and contribute more to their work and their companies; they are driven by their experience of meaning, value, and purpose in their work.
- Engagement is about putting discretionary effort into work—going above and beyond without extrinsic compensation or incentive. Engaged employees put forth more effort than their pay would elicit from unengaged employees.
- Engagement creates higher levels of performance in terms of safety, quality, patient experience, and profit.

CREATING ENGAGEMENT

Unlocking the secret to high levels of engagement for both leaders and team members begins with organizational leaders understanding and focusing on the fundamental needs of their people. People follow leaders for specific reasons. You already acknowledged this truth in the "best leader/worst boss" exercise from part I. When we survey people about what they need from an effective leader, they are able to describe these behaviors with extraordinary clarity. Gallup has also identified a clear set of fundamental human needs (Rath and Conchie 2008). To be an effective leader, it would benefit you greatly to learn and demonstrate behaviors that fulfill the legitimate needs of your team members daily. It is not rocket science, as the old saying goes; but it is brain science.

Trust

Trust and engagement are inseparable (Covey 2006). Without trust, leaders cannot make meaningful emotional connections with their team members. In the absence of those connections, performance deteriorates and people lose alignment between focusing on objectives and delivering key results—they lose engagement. Talk to a group of people struggling to produce results, and you will be talking with a group of people who are struggling to trust.

Neuroscientists have discovered that the hormone and neurotransmitter oxytocin increases a person's willingness to trust others. Oxytocin plays a key role in human social bonding, motivation, emotion, and reward. That is why oxytocin is such an influential trigger for upper brain performance factors—it creates collaborative relationships. When people are in a safe, nurturing environment, their brains release more oxytocin (Delgado 2008). Trust-earning behaviors that stimulate the release of oxytocin include the following:

- Consistency in manner, words, and actions.
- Accountability and transparency, including active listening.
- Sharing information and taking responsibility instead of blaming.
- Genuine interest in and concern for others.
- Respectful and equal regard for the core values of inclusion and diversity standards.
- Random acts of thoughtfulness and kindness.

Through his research on oxytocin (also shown to facilitate collaboration and teamwork), Paul J. Zak (2019) has developed a framework for creating a culture of trust and building a joyful, more loyal, and more engaged workforce. By calculating people's oxytocin levels in response to different situations—first in the lab and later in the workplace—Zak identified eight key performance behaviors leaders can use to stimulate oxytocin production, thereby generating trust and creating engagement:

1. Recognize excellence.
2. Induce challenge stress.
3. Give people discretion in how they do their work.
4. Enable job crafting, giving people more control over their work.
5. Share information openly and inclusively.
6. Intentionally build relationships and effective social networks.
7. Facilitate whole-person growth (spiritual, physical, emotional, and mental).
8. Show vulnerability—people must be able to identify with you to trust you.

A nonthreatening relationship is necessary for trust to grow. Behavior predictability in a leader promotes feelings of trust. Trusting a volatile leader is hard, especially in times of change. The connection between how the brain works and how we develop trust may be the reason it requires so much effort to rebuild a relationship damaged by the loss of trust. Essentially, our brains must be rewired to enable us to replace bad memories with caring experiences. This rewiring must be a mutual effort involving all people in the relationship. The good news is that trust, this very important intangible in life, can be built where it does not exist, increased where it is scarce, and regained where it was lost.

Compassion

Compassionate leaders are willing to acknowledge and work with their team members to overcome obstacles and challenges. Compassionate leaders care for people. Studies show that of the four fundamental human needs, expressing compassion may be the hardest performance behavior for leaders to acknowledge and demonstrate (Rath and Conchie 2009). The core research conducted at Gallup on compassion and engagement included interviewing more than 13 million people in the workplace. The key finding indicates that when people do not have close friendships on the job and a supervisor or leader who really cares about them individually, there is almost no chance that they will engage in their work.

In our neuroscience research, we have discovered that oxytocin plays a major role not only in building trust but also in expressing compassion—both to others and, perhaps most importantly, to oneself. Compassion extends beyond the feeling of empathy in the face of pain and suffering. Compassion is the outward expression of the inner feeling of empathy. When activated, oxytocin produces feelings of comfort and stability and is associated with enduring improvements in mood and well-being.

The upper brain connection with oxytocin stimulation enhances your ability to focus on things that really matter when you are experiencing stress, frustration, and conflict. Studies show that in acts of kindness and compassion, both you and the recipient of your goodwill receive a dose of oxytocin. Simply observing an act of compassion results in the same neurochemical stimulation and release of oxytocin (Samton 2017).

Performance behaviors that consistently reflect compassion are essential to creating engagement in an organization. Self-compassion, perhaps more popularly known as self-care, is equally valuable. Self-compassion is associated with lower rates of depression, self-criticism, and physical ailments, as well as improved immune system functioning. When we are experiencing self-compassion, we ask ourselves what we need to feel better and how we can minimize negative emotions.

We learn to give ourselves a sense of comfort and nurturing. Activating this response takes a lot of practice. Next time you notice you are experiencing distressing thoughts, practice the exercise included in the "Put It to Work" section at the end of this chapter to learn this important skill.

Security and Stability

Leaders must constantly strive to foster a sense of security and stability throughout their organization. These behaviors will stimulate the release of oxytocin, and people will engage with their work, be supportive of one another, and produce results at a higher level of performance. The other side of the coin is that leaders need to constantly analyze whether they are doing anything that creates insecurity and instability in their organization.

As soon as people begin to feel the loss of security and stability in the organization, they lose their engagement. When people lose their engagement, performance degrades quickly. Our brains cannot focus on growth, development, and performance if they are instead focusing on survival. The human brain is not a dual-core processor; it is highly efficient at upper-brain activity for performance and lower-brain activity for survival, but it cannot do both at the same time.

The neuroscientific evidence for this tension between the upper brain and lower brain tension is the stress response known as "fight, flight, or freeze," coined by American physiologist Walter Cannon (Lambert 2018). Stress responses, which are essential for survival, are managed by the sympathetic nervous system and the hypothalamic-pituitary-adrenal (HPA) axis. When activated by a threat stimulus such as the loss of security and stability, the HPA axis signals the release of the brain hormone cortisol. Cortisol plays a central role in managing the threat/stress response by mobilizing and shifting energy resources to increase arousal and alertness, enhance vigilance, and sharpen memory.

When you are experiencing stress, it is essential that your brain receive appropriate feedback to trigger cortisol release to manage your threat response. It is equally essential that your brain receive appropriate feedback once the threat has passed, so that baseline levels of cortisol are reestablished. We will discuss more of the specific functioning of the HPA axis and its physiological effect on your leadership effectiveness in chapter 6. It will suffice for now to understand that when people face long-term chronic insecurity and instability in the workplace, engagement and high performance are impossible. In the end, leaders are responsible for creating an environment that allows people's upper brains to work effectively for their well-being, engagement, and performance.

Hope

Hope and stability go hand in hand. Hope rests on the foundation of stability and security. When people find themselves in situations full of constant instability and insecurity, they eventually begin to lose hope. The "operating system" of their brain becomes infected with the virus of negativity. Left unchecked, this virus begins to make physical changes to their brain, disrupting their ability to connect and ignite their upper brain for performance. The worst aspect of this unending stream of conscious negativity is a condition the literature describes as *learned helplessness* (Cloud 2013).

The positive psychology movement deserves credit for advancing the science that demonstrates the physiological changes in the brain resulting from positive or negative thoughts. We previously discussed how a threatened brain responds with cortisol and how disruptive this brain hormone is to performance when chronically induced. These alterations of neurochemicals, along with associated neural networks of the brain, have long been implicated in depression. By cultivating hope through encouragement, leaders can reverse learned helplessness and lead the upper brains of their team members to higher levels of development, well-being, and performance.

Cognitive behavioral therapy has demonstrated high efficacy rates in managing causes of depression, anxiety, and learned helplessness. Martin Seligman and Steve Maier's research in the 1960s produced a theory on learned helplessness that both now declare was wrong. It is hopelessness—not helplessness—that undermines mental health and resilience. Researching a neurochemical connection to depression in the 1980s led to an understanding of how serotonin levels affect hopefulness, and even demonstrated a link to the symptoms of depression. Hope, then, is the antidote for the negativity and discouragement virus. Hope provides the means to rewrite brain software and rewire a person's upper brain operating system.

The greatest gift that leaders can give their team members is hope. Hope gives people purpose and a reason to commit to their jobs and their organizations. Without trust, compassion, security, and stability, duplicating hope's aspirational effects is nearly impossible. Without hope, creating engagement is nearly impossible, too. Hope is one of the most powerful forces in the universe. You need hope to attract people to the organization's vision and lead them toward a better future.

Cultivating hope has always been a critical aspect of effective leadership. Arguably, it may be the single most important thing you can do as a leader to create engagement, focus on the well-being of your people, and drive performance. In the research of hope and the powerful effect it has on human lives, the literature identifies four primary responses to hope (Johnston 2014):

1. *Liberation.* Hope sets you free from your past. Your past need not be a determining factor for your future. Whatever choices led to your current circumstances, you can create a hopeful future with more effective choices in the present. Hope will even free you from low expectations and a stifling lack of self-confidence.

2. *Motivation.* Everyone experiences difficulties, challenges, and pain in their life. Resilience is a key ingredient in the lives of people who thrive in agonizing situations and is lacking in those who decline into learned helplessness. Hope helps you bounce back and strengthens and reinforces resilience. Expressing thanks, having a heart of gratitude, and seeking to find something positive in the midst of the most discouraging circumstances will keep you filled with hope. Hope will keep you motivated to persevere in the darkest days until the sun starts to shine in your life again.

3. *Inspiration.* Hope sets you free to dream *big* dreams. If you cannot dream the impossible, then you can never achieve it. Hope gives birth to dreams that create momentum to take action. Look at the lives of the most positive and memorable leaders in your lifetime. They all share the attribute of hope. Martin Luther King Jr. said, "I have a dream." The hope he carried in his heart became the inspiration for the dream that changed the world for the better.

4. *Activation.* Hope is the perpetual force for creating and sustaining growth and innovation. Hope is the catalyst that drives creative thinking and continuous performance improvement. Hope allows you to believe that you can change a negative situation into a positive one by taking action. Hope is the sustaining quality that helps people believe that, regardless of the circumstances, they can be a force for good in the world. It is amazing to see the difference that can be made in the world by people who are sustained by hope.

Perhaps the greatest challenge facing business leaders is to create the kind of culture and organizational atmosphere that promotes trust, compassion, security, and hope. Future historians may well judge our organizations (and society as a whole) based on whether they were able to fulfill these four fundamental human needs. Will those historians find that we treated people with integrity and trust, united people in compassionate service, fostered security and stability, and offered encouragement and hope whenever possible, finding ways to uphold the inherent worth and value of everyone?

CONSEQUENCES OF DISENGAGEMENT

When leaders fail to foster engagement within their organizations, they risk creating a perfect storm for disengagement and its more destructive variant—burnout. Christina Maslach is an American social psychologist and professor emerita of psychology at the University of California, Berkeley, known for her research on engagement and occupational burnout. Her work on this subject is likely the most extensive in the field, covering multiple decades. The consistent findings of the collective body of work in this field reflect the following consequences of disengagement and burnout (Riley 2020; Schelenz 2020):

- *Decreased productivity.* Disengaged employees put forth less effort on the job, are less motivated to fulfill basic expectations, and contribute to increased frequency of errors and quality problems. Most actively disengaged employees are more interested in finding new employment than in performing at high levels in their current position. The resulting decreases in quality and performance and increases in turnover can be costly.

- *Poor customer (patient) experiences.* Organizations with lower customer experience scores generally have lower employee engagement scores as well. In contrast, organizations with above-average customer experience scores tend to report much higher employee engagement scores as well—an average of 79 percent according to one study.

- *Lower levels of performance.* Disengaged employees drag down their colleagues' productivity and morale, damage customer relationships, and make it harder (or impossible) for the organization to meet its goals. "Disengaged employees have the power to break an organization" (Riley 2020).

- *Human costs.* Burnout happens when emotional exhaustion, physical exhaustion, and a loss of meaning in a person's work come together. The human cost happens when people feel overwhelmed, emotionally drained, and unable to respond to the demands of personal and professional obligations (Frisina 2017). Workplace stress is estimated to cost the US economy more than $500 billion a year. Caregivers such as doctors and nurses are especially vulnerable to burnout, which contributes to tremendously high suicide rates in these professions: Men who are primary care providers have a 40 percent higher risk of suicide, while for women the risk is 130 percent higher.

Maslach revolutionized the study of burnout by developing the Maslach Burnout Inventory, which provides a way to measure the symptoms of burnout. The assessment is organized around three dimensions: emotional exhaustion, depersonalization, and sense (or lack) of personal accomplishment. When a person is burned out, these dimensions correlate to exhaustion, negativity or cynicism, and a sense of professional ineffectiveness. The assessment identifies a spectrum of five groups of people, ranging from engagement (positive in all three dimensions) to burnout (negative in all three dimensions). The other three profiles—overextended, ineffective, and disengaged—describe different combinations of positive and negative dimensions.

People who are overextended or ineffective can benefit from resilience training and have reasonable expectations of joining the ranks of the engaged members of an organization. People who are disengaged or burned out suffer from high levels of cynicism, making it more difficult to overcome the obstacles to change (Frisina 2017). Ideally, with effective coaching and support from colleagues and managers, they could find a new beginning at work. The hope for disengaged people is that they have the energy to try something new. Recovery from burnout presents greater challenges because those experiencing burnout feel frustrated and lack the energy and confidence that would contribute to an effective response for change.

The World Health Organization adopted Maslach's conception of burnout and is developing guidelines to help organizations manage the problem. Consequently, it is becoming more commonly accepted that fixing this chronic workplace problem is a fundamental responsibility of organizational leaders, and is not up to the individual members of the organization.

Organizations with high engagement benefit from a culture that produces increased employee retention, increased employee performance, and increased employee loyalty and well-being (chapter 5). The pathway to high-level organizational performance is founded on effective leadership and employee engagement. Effective leadership behaviors (chapter 6) are the catalyst that allows organizational members to connect to and ignite their upper brains for growth, well-being, and performance. Members of an organization who function from their upper brain are fully engaged. When employees are engaged they are more likely to invest in the work they do, which leads to the production of higher-quality work. Engaged organizations are twice as successful as less-engaged organizations (Baldoni 2013).

Remember, engaged employees love their jobs. They seek personal, continuous performance improvement. They are constantly seeking ways to make themselves better and to improve the performance of their organizations. Engaged employees are always waiting on an effective leader to lead their upper brains to levels of performance excellence. You can be that kind of effective leader.

KEY TAKEAWAYS

- Superior results do not happen without an engaged workforce. An engaged workforce does not happen without effective leadership. It is simple neuroscience that the human brain works from achievement drivers on the one hand and survival drivers on the other.

- You can, in your own behavior, nurture positive connections with members of your team to create and cultivate engagement and drive performance.

- Talk to a group of people struggling to produce results, and you will be talking to a group of people who are struggling to trust.

- When trust is absent, damaged, or lost in the workplace, relationships are dysfunctional and work effectiveness and performance suffer.

- By cultivating hope through encouragement, leaders can reverse learned helplessness and lead the upper brains of their team members to higher levels of development, well-being, and performance.

- When leaders fail to foster engagement within their organizations, they risk creating a perfect storm for disengagement and its more destructive variant—burnout.

- The pathway to high-level organizational performance is founded on effective leadership and employee engagement.

PUT IT TO WORK

1. Do you share information (positive or negative) that is helpful to others, or do you withhold it? Similarly, does your team share relevant information? If not, what is keeping all or some of you from practicing transparency?

2. Do you treat everyone with kindness, respect, and compassion? Similarly, how do your team members treat each other? What are the social norms in your team?

3. Do you follow through on your commitments, even if you do so at considerable personal expense? How do you hold your team to the same level of accountability?

4. Why do you consider yourself a trustworthy person? Which members of your team display trustworthy behavior? How do you highlight the ideal behaviors of your team members so that others may learn from them or emulate them?

5. When you experience distressing thoughts, try this exercise to stimulate oxytocin release (created by The Heart Math Institute: www.heartmath.com/quick-coherence-technique/):

   • First, focus your attention in the area of the heart. Imagine your breath is flowing in and out of your heart or chest area, breathing a little slower and deeper than usual. Suggestion: Inhale five seconds, exhale five seconds (or whatever rhythm is comfortable).

   • Then, make a sincere attempt to experience a regenerative feeling such as appreciation or care for someone or something in your life. Suggestion: Try to re-experience the feeling you have for someone or something you love—a pet, a special place, an accomplishment—or focus on a feeling of calm or ease.

6. We recommend, with no financial interest, information for the Maslach Burnout Inventory available from Mind Garden (www.mindgarden.com/117-maslach-burnout-inventory-mbi). We have used it with our clients to achieve high levels of consistency in a comprehensive review of all the five key groups of the performance

spectrum. Remember, you cannot change what you do not manage, and you cannot manage what you do not know. This assessment tool will be beneficial in developing your engagement strategies.

REFERENCES

Baldoni, J. 2013. "Employee Engagement Does More Than Boost Productivity." *Harvard Business Review*. Published July 4. https://hbr.org/2013/07/employee-engagement-does-more.

Cloud, H. 2013. *Boundaries for Leaders: Results, Relationships, and Being Ridiculously in Charge*. New York: HarperCollins.

Covey, S. M. R. 2006. *The Speed of Trust: The One Thing That Changes Everything*. New York: Free Press.

Delgado, M. 2008. "To Trust or Not to Trust: Ask Oxytocin." *Scientific American*. Published July 15. www.scientificamerican.com/article/to-trust-or-not-to-trust/.

Frisina, M. 2017. "Strategies for Reversing and Eliminating Physician Burnout." *Management in Healthcare* 2 (3): 254–63.

Gallup. 2021. "What Is Employee Engagement?" Accessed October 19. www.gallup.com/workplace/285674/improve-employee-engagement-workplace.aspx#ite-285701.

George, B. 2003. *Authentic Leadership: Rediscovering the Secrets to Creating Lasting Value*. San Francisco: Jossey-Bass.

Goleman, D., R. Boyaztzis, and A. McKee. 2013. *Primal Leadership: Unleashing the Power of Emotional Intelligence*. Boston: Harvard Business Review Press.

Johnston, R. 2014. *The Hope Quotient: Measure It. Raise It. You'll Never Be the Same*. Nashville, TN: W Publishing Group.

Lambert, K. 2018. *Biological Psychology*. New York: Oxford University Press.

Morse, G. 2003. "Why We Misread Motives." *Harvard Business Review*. Published January. https://hbr.org/2003/01/why-we-misread-motives.

Rath, T., and B. Conchie. 2009. "What Followers Want from Leaders." *Gallup Business Journal*. Published January 8. https://news.gallup.com/businessjournal/113542/what-followers-want-from-leaders.aspx.

———. 2008. *Strengths Based Leadership: Great Leaders, Teams, and Why People Follow*. New York: Gallup Press.

Riley, J. F. 2020. "How Disengaged Employees Affect Your Organization." GuideSpark (blog). Updated June 5. www.guidespark.com/blog/how-disengaged-employees-affect-your-organization/.

Samton, J. 2017. "The Neuroscience of Building Compassion and Resilience." *Inc*. Published March 12. www.inc.com/julia-samton/the-neuroscience-of-compassion.html.

Schelenz, R. 2020. "Job Burnout Is a Billion-Dollar Program. Can We Fix It, Despite COVID-19?" *University of California News*. Published September 3. www.universityofcalifornia.edu/news/job-burnout-billion-dollar-problem-can-we-fix-it-despite-covid-19.

Zak, P. 2019. "How Our Brains Decide When to Trust." *Harvard Business Review*. Published July 18. https://hbr.org/2019/07/how-our-brains-decide-when-to-trust.

CHAPTER 5

Creating a Culture of Purpose and Performance

If you are lucky enough to be someone's employer, then you have a moral obligation to make sure people do look forward to coming to work in the morning.

—John Mackey

WE CAN LEARN many leadership lessons from the Space Race between the United States and the former Soviet Union to put the first astronaut on the moon. The Soviet Union started with a string of early achievements, while NASA was still in its formative stages:

- The first satellite in space.
- The first dog in space.
- The first probe to impact the moon.
- The first astronaut to orbit the earth and return safely.

During this time, NASA toiled under its own start-up programs and produced one ill-fated rocket launch after another. When

President Kennedy gave his famous "We choose to go the moon" speech, it was clear to many within NASA that the American space program was not prepared to achieve this objective. What vaulted this fledgling space program from a series of catastrophic errors to successfully outpacing its competitor to send a team of US astronauts to land on—and safely return from—the surface of the moon?

The turnaround began in 1963, when engineer George Mueller was named the head of NASA's Office of Manned Space Flight. Mueller was not an aerospace or aeronautical engineer; when he was appointed, his resume included nothing about working with rockets. He was an electrical engineer, and accordingly had a profound knowledge of complex systems and processes. He also understood the value of organizational culture to drive performance.

One of the first things Mueller did was consolidate the manned spacecraft, flight, and launch operations offices. Another key undertaking was a complete reorganization of the direct reporting chain for each of the critical program project leaders. Each functional program now had a manager and direct report. Mueller then created conceptual awareness for this leadership dyad about how the work of each functional project connected and contributed to the overall mission of the entire space program. In a systematic and science-based approach to outcomes, Mueller created a reporting chain that had a clear vision, clear objectives, and clear accountability for outcomes.

One of Mueller's most innovative practices was the mass sharing of information across NASA. He improved and enhanced access to and dissemination of information into a set of expanded communication networks throughout the organization. Before the internet, the ability to rapidly share information within a highly complex organization was always a performance challenge. Mueller created an integrated radio system that allowed individual managers and engineers to share information with one another in real time. Leaders could respond to significant unplanned events with greater effectiveness and efficiency, changing the overall outcome of the event.

In short, Mueller was able to create a dynamic, collaborative performance culture within NASA—an organization that included over 300,000 members, 200 universities, and 20,000 contractors. In less than six years he transformed a fledgling and fragmented space program into a performance juggernaut that propelled the first astronauts to the moon. Mueller knew that a culture of collaboration—shared vision, common goals, and mutual support among team members—was the critical element to connect people with common objectives and produce results at a high level of performance outcomes.

THE IMPACT OF CULTURE ON ENGAGEMENT

What is so profound about NASA's transformation is Mueller's decision to focus on creating a robust culture of performance excellence before developing a strategic plan. A performance culture creates the organization's environment and influences the nature of the long-term plans that move the organization toward its vision. A performance culture also dictates the policies and processes that enable the organization to live its mission every day. Ultimately, this kind of performance culture also enhances the growth, development, and value of members of the organization, whose contributions to achievement bring meaning and purpose to their work.

In an organization with a functional culture and effective leadership, employees demonstrate three key elements of engaged performance behaviors:

1. A clear sense of purpose.
2. Understanding of immediate and long-term goals.
3. Commitment to furthering the objectives of the organization.

In other words, the organization's leadership and culture becomes the engine behind the organization's engagement capacity to drive performance. We are amazed at the number of leaders we meet who continue to prioritize strategy over culture, plan over people, and process over relationships in high-performing teams and still expect to achieve results when the data say otherwise.

Yet more evidence of the importance of the human elements of organizations came in the late 1980s and early 1990s; between half and three-quarters of the mergers and reengineering and restructuring projects undertaken in this period failed. These expensive experiences taught change management experts to share slogans such as "Culture beats strategy." We have not seen a significant change in the science of performance management over the last 15 years; so we are not suggesting that you neglect or disregard the planning process and development of strategic plans. Rather, we ask you to remember that organizational culture is a group of internal values and behaviors in an organization. It includes experiences, ways of thinking, beliefs, and expectations. Culture is also intuitive, involving repetitive habits and emotional responses. Organizational culture affects the emotional center of the brain and can override its cognitive functioning. Culture beats strategy every time because emotions beat logic every time. Regardless of what innovative strategy you develop for your organization, when the culture is dysfunctional—when people are disengaged and do not connect to the strategy in daily performance—the strategy fails.

We do well to remember these wise words from Mark Fields, former CEO of Ford Motor Company: "You can have the best plan in the world, and if the culture isn't going to let it happen, it's going to die on the vine" (Durbin 2006). Culture still beats strategy when it comes to engaged teams and organizational performance. You get in performance outcomes and results what you create or what you allow in your leadership behavior. Remember that when leaders begin to behave differently—more effectively— most of the problems that are corrupting organizational culture and hindering engaged performance go away.

CULTURE AND THE MOBILE WORKFORCE

Gone are the days when a paycheck, the employee-of-the-month award, and the gold watch at retirement were considered sufficient motivators for people to perform at their best and to remain dedicated to an organization. Even before the COVID-19 pandemic, many organizations were making the transition to knowledge-based organizational cultures that include all the dynamics and inherent challenges of a mobile workforce, with employees connected by technology such as computers, smartphones, and other mobile devices instead of restricted to a central physical location. The idea of a mobile workforce goes well beyond simply working from home. It also means people can live remotely, in places that are considerable distances from what would have been a traditional physical work location.

Technology has also changed how businesses provide their products and services. Even in healthcare, technological advances and social-distancing requirements enhanced and improved the practice of telehealth and telemedicine, as well as home health care, known as "technology-based care provider house calls."

Healthcare leaders will face a considerable challenge in matching job requirements to constantly changing technology. They will also have the challenge of matching job requirements to employee preferences for mobile working. More than 70 percent of the workforce will be millennials or younger by 2030 (Shein 2021). Younger employees expect instant access to information and more mobile opportunities.

Just as technology has increased the borders of our markets, it has also increased competition for the best and brightest employees. Employees today seek to work for organizations and leaders they can be proud of and who treat them like active contributors, not passive producers. The Society for Human Resource Management (SHRM 2020) reports that "relationships with immediate supervisor" rank as more significant to employees than benefits or the organization's financial stability. Employees want to work for leaders who appreciate the value they add to performance—their passions and talents—to every extent possible, which is a key part of the definition of knowledge-based workers.

Businesses, governments, public institutions, and health-care delivery systems can all take advantage of mobile flexibility. Following are just some of the many advantages of these new opportunities:

- Reduced employee stress from removing the pressure of a daily commute while providing an easier work–life balance, which can translate into higher productivity and fewer sick days.
- Improved business continuity from having mobile-based employees continue working to sustain critical operational functions if a company experiences downtime from a disaster.
- Deterrence of discrimination and encouragement of diversity as a result of choosing a workforce from a variety of geographic locations, enhancing socioeconomic and cultural diversity.

Effective leaders will acknowledge the societal shifts that require altering workplace cultures and leadership behaviors. One direct effect on workplace culture is the degree to which individual leaders choose to engage with their team members. As leaders, we must make a purposeful decision to engage our employees. Ultimately, engagement is a personal matter.

Each of us has a responsibility to apply learning and development methods in a personal quest to improve how we engage with our work and the performance outcomes we produce. Effective leaders who acquire and consistently practice a behavior skill set that creates a culture promoting personal ownership, accountability, and responsibility in their team members are the necessary variable in the performance formula.

BAD APPLES AND BAD BARRELS

Many of us have heard that one bad apple can spoil the barrel. This timeless adage relates to the negative effects that some behaviors can have on results. Many of us have used this metaphor to illustrate the need to avoid bringing toxic individuals into our teams and workplaces. In virtually every organization and team, there is one individual universally regarded as detrimental to the unity and harmony of team relationships. These "bad apples" are detrimental to the execution of the mission, vision, values, and strategies of the organization, as well.

It costs about $4,425 to recruit and hire an employee, and more than three times that if they are an executive (SHRM 2017). You do not want to make the mistake of hiring an employee who will be disruptive in the workplace—someone who comes to work every day intent on being disruptive and uncooperative. No organization needs a team member like this. If employees exhibit toxic behavior, the organization will also exhibit toxic behavior. When you avoid hiring a toxic employee, you save about $12,500 in lost productivity and impaired morale (Vozza 2020).

The reverse of this principle is also true. Hiring great talent and then having them work for a toxic boss in a toxic culture is just as costly, in terms of real dollars, as hiring toxic employees. Doing so is also costly in human terms, causing increased negative stress, anxiety, and other work-related illnesses that affect performance (Schwantes 2020). Toxic behaviors, whether displayed by a boss or a coworker, are observable and measurable. Following are the most common toxic behaviors affecting team members' ability to engage in their work:

- *Narcissism.* Narcissists lack empathy, have a strong desire to break rules and defy the status quo, and are likely to engage in manipulation to advance themselves at the expense of others. "Life is all about me and don't you ever forget it" is the narcissist's motto.

- *Micromanagement.* Toxic people are highly independent to the point of exclusion. They lack the desire to work within the legitimate boundaries of a team, and constantly meddle in the work responsibilities of other people. They have a hard time letting go and trusting their team members to perform their work. The employee experience under such suffocating micromanagement can be downright demoralizing.

- *Setting unrealistic expectations.* Effective leaders establish high standards and stretch goals, encouraging team members to strive for higher levels of performance. They are always coaching and encouraging their team members on this journey to continuous performance improvement. Toxic bosses can sabotage the workplace with unachievable goals and unrealistic expectations. Toxic bosses set up their team members to fail and then shame and blame them. Working in this kind of toxic culture creates a wave of negative emotions, leaving employees feeling disengaged and hopeless.

- *Rudeness.* In meetings, toxic bosses and coworkers may interrupt their team members who present a perspective or idea that does not align with their own. Toxic bosses and coworkers may deliberately shut others down when they feel threatened by differing points of view. Toxic people will spread gossip; they disrupt communication among team members and show contempt for others through a lack of basic courtesies.

- *Behavior incompetence.* Toxic people display fundamental incompetence in basic interpersonal relationship skills. This behavior incompetence often stems from arrogance and overconfidence in their level of technical skill, talent, and intellect.

Companies spend billions of dollars annually on leadership development training. Yet, toxic leadership and the perpetuation of toxic cultures continue at alarming rates.

Consider the following: Despite the $15 billion companies spend annually on managerial and leadership development, toxic bosses are common in the American workforce. A study by Life Meets Work found that 56 percent of American workers claim their boss is mildly or highly toxic. A study by the American Psychological Association found that 75 percent of Americans say their "boss is the most stressful part of their workday" (Abbajay 2018). When you bring high-performing, intelligent people into a toxic culture, their level of engagement and performance behavior will be a direct reflection of the workplace culture you created and allowed.

As leaders, we must be able to identify toxic members of our organizations. We must also be introspective enough to recognize whether we, as leaders, are creating or have created a toxic environment that hinders the team unity and harmony necessary for high-level performance. This is why the key indicator of organizational effectiveness is individual leader behavior.

Creating a culture of achievement and performance is an intentional undertaking that requires time and dedication. The payoff, however, is immeasurable. Here are three key attributes we have discovered in organizations that have successfully developed cultures that foster high levels of engagement:

1. Consistently setting and achieving challenging goals.
2. Communicating positive expectations about success.
3. Demonstrating that they value their employees and want them to succeed.

Whether the problem is toxic people or a toxic culture, we must recognize that negative workplace behaviors drive negative performance outcomes. In healthcare organizations, toxic workplace behaviors harm patients, drag down morale, and create a negative work atmosphere. This type of environment will not bring people together to create anything of value. The appropriate response is to create a culture of engagement and collaboration. Without it, negative competition and conflict reign—two conditions in which medical errors are likely to occur. When staff morale and motivation are low, performance is inconsistent and unreliable, and communication and cooperation are nonexistent. Who wants to work in this kind of environment? For that matter, who wants to be a consumer in this kind of environment?

GENERATIONAL GAPS AND CULTURE

Today's workforce spans five generations, with Generation Z—the largest demographic cohort in the United States, at more than 60 million strong—about to join the party (Gayle 2019). A 2018 Deloitte survey found that many of the performance drivers associated with previous age cohorts do not motivate many of these young people in today's workforce. Deloitte surveyed more than 10,000 degree-holding millennials in 36 countries who were employed full-time in large, private-sector organizations. Almost half (43%) said they planned to leave their jobs within two years; less than a third (28%) expected to stay beyond five years (Brinded 2018). One office space consultant noted that some companies are making changes to workplace environments, even in lighting and color schemes, to make these groups more comfortable: "Simple changes can be made without catering to just one group. Rethinking of colors, making sure acoustics and audio technology makes provision for those harder of hearing and introducing (and allowing) easy access to mother's rooms are some of the easy wins which won't impact the office overall, but will cater to an aging workforce" (Inspiration Office 2018).

Together with the research we conduct, this information suggests that leaders must be purposeful and intentional about managing organizational dynamics such as culture, generational gaps, and brand image. These dynamics are not problems to be solved, but states of nature that require constant attention.

How clients, customers, and patients experience the external effects of your organizational culture is a byproduct of how your employees experience the internal effects of your organizational culture. As Tony Hsieh, former CEO of Zappos, famously said, "Your culture is your brand." And in any organization, that culture is driven and created as a direct result of the level of engagement you have as leader in your organization.

Generational engagement is not a new concept. The baby boomers of the 1960s became the "suits" of the 1990s. Currently, many millennials are becoming leaders in their organizations. How we sustain performance and success in our organizations is how people will identify with and cultivate the core values, ethics, and workplace culture that we, as leaders, choose to create. If you want a dynamic, healthy, performance-driven culture, you have to create it. As Henry Cloud and others have written so eloquently, you, as a leader, are ridiculously in charge. You receive in performance outcomes what you create or allow in your culture. You can only create and sustain culture through purposeful efforts of leadership. Either you create the culture you desire, or the culture will take on a life of its own.

In the last ten years, we have seen too much of millennial blame and its effect on workplace performance. Performance is leadership's responsibility, and there has not been enough effort by leaders to create the workplace culture that enables millennials—and now Generation Z team members—to engage with and thrive in their work.

A CULTURE BUILT FOR PERFORMANCE

In today's professional world, people crave effective leadership. Many analysts misattribute performance deficiencies to generational gaps; however, those performance deficiencies could well be attributed to midlevel managers and their team members being overburdened and uninspired by leaders who are failing to provide effective leadership or effective management. "People do not resist change. They resist being changed" (Senge 2010, 144). Knowledge-based workers desire leadership that capitalizes on collaboration, communication, and connection to accomplish their work-related goals and objectives.

One of the key behaviors of an effective leader who is able to connect and engage with others is practicing followership. *Followership* is a leader's willingness to listen to those for whom they are responsible. On engagement surveys, employees choose "listening to me" as the highest-rated attribute of an effective leader. Leadership literature emphasizes the need for leaders to talk in ways that will make people want to listen. We believe it is equally important for leaders to listen in ways that will make others want to speak to them.

Effective listening creates a connection between the leader and the legitimate needs and desires of team members. By paying attention to members of the team through active listening, a leader gains information and insight into the factors that drive performance. Although followership is a concept written about in reputable business journals and several books, the idea is still a novelty to many in titled positions of authority (Peters and Haslem 2018).

People do not quit their jobs. They quit the cultures their leaders have created. As human beings, "*why* we work determines how *well* we work" (McGregor and Doshi 2015). If you have fostered a negative or toxic culture, then you can expect your top performers to leave, or to stick around while putting in the minimal amount of effort necessary to keep their jobs. Ineffective leaders breed ineffective followers; performance and productivity suffer as a result. Having a positive, emotional connection with your people sends a clear message—that you are interested and invested in what your people experience on a daily basis.

People, in general, do not follow just anyone, nor do they follow out of the goodness of their hearts. They need good reasons—motivation—to follow. You are responsible for giving them those reasons by understanding what they want and need to fulfill their work requirements and contribute to a mutually beneficial and meaningful purpose in their work. Culture is the set of processes in an organization that affects the overall motivation of its people. In a high-performing culture, those processes maximize overall motivation.

Edward Deci and Richard Ryan of the University of Rochester identified six main reasons people work: play, purpose, potential, emotional pressure, economic pressure, and inertia (McGregor and Doshi 2015). Each of these six reasons is directly tied to the way the upper brain functions. For example, the upper brain provides the capacity for creativity and imagination. That is where key elements of innovation have their origin. Deci and Ryan's concept of playfulness describes the way people work to create something new as a form of human discovery and natural curiosity.

Meaning, value, and purpose are also upper brain qualities. Purpose adds meaning to work. When people fail to engage in their work with purpose, work simply becomes a means to an end—earning income. People are engaged, driven to fulfill the objectives of their teams and their organization, when their work has purpose. You cannot connect to purpose in your work and live life in your lower brain.

Potential involves upper brain functions when we seek to discover something new. As we discussed in part I, learning, growth, and personal improvement all result in positive brain stimulation. That is why we seek to maximize our potential and obtain peak performance in most important activities in which we engage as human beings.

We have already discussed the key role emotions have in guiding behavior in both the upper and lower brains. Emotional pressure has both a positive and negative effect on how leaders affect the brains of their people, particularly people's work motivation and engagement. Competitiveness and ambition are positive emotional pressures that provide motivation to work at high levels of performance. Conversely, emotional pressure based on fear or unhealthy competitive cultures manifest lower brain behaviors, severely degrading performance.

Finally, economic pressure and inertia can both be diagnosed based on predictive upper brain and lower brain behaviors unique to everyone's behavior patterns. Gaining rewards and achievement are both positive motivators for work. Taking initiative and redefining the *why* of what you do at work, and not merely what you do, happens when you are working from your upper brain.

People still want to make a difference at work. They want to feel inspired by what they do; they want to be inspired by their leader. Today's newest workers seek intrinsic value in their jobs beyond just paychecks. They want leaders who will give them control and empower them to do their jobs and solve problems. For some of you, giving away control may seem like a radical idea and a deviation from the historical top-down approach to leadership. However, if you want to connect, if you want to become an effective leader, then you have to discard the outdated and ineffective practices of the past that limit your leadership capacity. As leaders we should be asking ourselves daily, Is my behavior drawing people toward me or pushing people away from me? Understanding what endears us to our team members is essential to understanding the great power of that connection to drive performance in the workplace.

ESTABLISHING TRUST AND CONNECTION TO CULTURE

Significant leadership change initiatives often focus on technology and process. Unfortunately, they frequently neglect the key ingredient for execution—the people of the organization. Think back to the beginning of this chapter and the story of George Mueller. NASA's overall performance achievements under Mueller's leadership were a combination of technical skill and culture.

Regardless of the industry, leaders must accept that engaged people are the most valuable organizational asset that drives performance. Organizations do not get things done; people do. For most people, understanding the why behind change initiatives is far more important than the what or how. Most people come to work with the desire to make a difference. When organizations focus on aligning people with strategy, the likelihood of successful performance outcomes improves.

In healthcare, as in many other industries, we continue to experience constant changes in process, technology, and regulatory oversight. The fundamental challenge for all leaders seems to remain constant—as a leader, how do you guide your organization through the constant changes driven by the market and other unpredictable factors to the desired outcomes? The answer is the development of an engaged, adaptable, and resilient workforce. Leadership is the daily expression of behaviors that encourage people to achieve the organization's purpose.

The fundamental principle we teach about leadership is that individual leader behavior is the single most important predictor of sustained, high-level organizational performance. We know this to be true because time and again we see people who are positively engaged in their work because they are positively connected to and engaged with their leaders.

Effective leaders succeed where other leaders fail because they perform at a higher level, are more productive, and achieve greater results than other leaders when faced with similar circumstances and given the same resources. The success of effective leaders is driven by what is commonly referred to as *performance capacity*, which is a set of performance behaviors that enables these leaders to become role models for followers, guide operational improvements, execute on strategy consistently, and sustain performance excellence.

Effective leaders recognize the importance of self-awareness, collaboration, and building highly effective relationships. They spend time focusing their efforts in key areas that will build connections with the people they lead to drive performance and create a culture of purpose. When you have a meaningful relationship with another person, you work more effectively together. You have a common goal and a consistent purpose. Your efforts are channeled toward a common outcome, and you drive performance in the organization to peak levels. The effectiveness of these relationships is based on the following performance behaviors:

- Consistency in manner, words, and actions.
- Accountability and transparency, including active listening, sharing information, and taking responsibility as the leader.
- Expressing genuine interest in and concern for others.
- Respectful and equal regard for and treatment of others, regardless of rank, position, or differences in human characteristics.
- Focused attention.
- Principled and evidence-based decision-making.
- Dedication to fulfilling (not just making) promises.
- Willingness to celebrate and reward exceptional work.

These behaviors are observable evidence of effective leadership. As masters of interpersonal relationships, effective leaders know that their everyday words, actions, and habits can either strengthen or weaken relationships that are fundamental to engagement. People can only take so much bad behavior before they lose their willingness to trust and begin to feel disconnected from their leaders and organizations. We can all list the outcomes of an unmotivated, disengaged workforce, particularly in high-stress and high-risk environments. This is why effective leaders are vigilant about exhibiting behaviors that foster engagement to drive performance outcomes.

Leaders, regardless of technical specialties or industry, cannot effectively implement systems and processes, no matter how well designed, redesigned, or improved, without a culture of purpose and performance. We are our own worst enemies in our zeal to change processes and systems while failing to account for human performance behavior. We virtually guarantee noncompliant behavior during the implementation of any new and improved process if we fail to account for the previous noncompliant behavior in the old, now-defunct process.

To add insult to injury we then go and purchase the next generation of improvement programs, focusing on reeducation and retraining initiatives. We are confident that a new program and more training will solve our performance problems, when the root cause is the lack of effective leadership behaviors. It would be a great tragedy for your organization to miss out on the opportunity to make significant improvements in safety, quality, and service because of fundamental behavior flaws and the misapplication of continuous performance improvement methodologies. We need to accept the fact that in the balance of our cultural ecosystems, we cannot create a technology or reengineer a process to compensate for our own unwillingness to change our behavior.

Stephen Covey (1999, 253) wrote that "approaching quality from the human side harmonizes systems with processes, unleashes latent creativity and energy, and creates other benefits that go right to the bottom line." Constancy of purpose and performance behaviors drive performance improvement and should be our starting point in creating this harmony, a new vision, and a sense of purpose for *why* we do *what* we do in healthcare—taking care of one another organizationally so we can take better care of our patients individually.

THE BOTTOM LINE

Creating a culture of purpose and performance excellence begins with effective leadership and requires you to understand yourself. You have to assess where you are so you can get better. The ancient aphorism "Know thyself" has been attributed to at least six Greek sages, the most notable being the philosopher Socrates. You may be familiar with the Latin version—*temet nosce*—which hung above the Oracle's door in the *Matrix* film series. Suffice it to say, virtually every kind of performance problem is caused by relationship dysfunction that stems from a lack of effective leadership behavior. Our quirky traits and habits, which we often cannot see, affect the people around us.

Effective leaders are aware of their behavior tendencies and preferences. They know how to manage their emotions, and they are keenly aware of the need to be highly skilled in social management, to create and sustain highly effective interpersonal relationships. They are empathic, in that they can sense the emotional states of other people, and they are compassionate in their behavior, seeking to acknowledge the legitimate needs of others. Until you can adopt and practice these kinds of effective leadership behaviors, you will have a constant challenge in creating highly engaged performance behaviors in your team members and getting the results you desire as a leader.

KEY TAKEAWAYS

- In a systematic and science-based approach to outcomes, effective leaders create a performance structure with a clear vision, clear objectives, and clear accountability for outcomes.
- Regardless of what innovative strategy you develop for your organization, when the culture is dysfunctional—when people are disengaged and do not connect to the strategy in daily performance—the strategy fails.
- Healthcare leaders will face a considerable challenge in seeking to match job requirements to constantly changing technology.
- Each of us has a responsibility to apply learning and development methods in a personal quest to improve how we engage with our work and the performance outcomes we produce.

- How clients, customers, and patients experience the external effects of your organizational culture is a byproduct of how your employees experience the internal effects of your organizational culture.

- Leadership literature places an emphasis on the need for leaders to talk in ways that will make people listen. We believe it is equally important for leaders to listen in such a way that will make others want to speak to them.

- We need to accept the fact that in the balance of our cultural ecosystems we cannot create a technology or reengineer a process to compensate for our own unwillingness to change our behavior.

- Regardless of the industry, leaders must accept that engaged people are the most valuable organizational asset that drives performance.

- Virtually every kind of performance problem is caused by relationship dysfunction that stems from a lack of effective leadership behavior. Our quirky traits and habits, which we often cannot see, affect the people around us.

PUT IT TO WORK

1. You will never lead other people successfully—influentially—if you do not lead yourself well. Benjamin Franklin wrote, "A man wrapped up in himself makes a very small bundle." Would you follow you as a leader? Are you the kind of leader others want to follow?

2. How much of your weekly time do you invest connecting with others and strengthening those connections? How is your current behavior benefiting the quality of your relationships?

3. How do you evaluate your own behavior and performance? How do you enable others to evaluate you?

What have you learned about yourself to this point in your reading? What are you willing to change as a result of this knowledge?

4. What is the level of empowerment within your team? Are team members allowed to make decisions regarding their respective roles and responsibilities? Are guidelines in place for team members to follow regarding decisions they are allowed (or not allowed) to make?

5. What is the level of blame and blame shifting in your culture? What part does blame play in team conflict or team challenges? What have you and your team done to resolve these issues? Were your efforts effective? If not, why not?

REFERENCES

Abbajay, M. 2018. "What to Do When You Have a Bad Boss." *Harvard Business Review*. Published September 7. https://hbr.org/2018/09/what-to-do-when-you-have-a-bad-boss.

Brinded, L. 2018. "Money Will Attract Millennials to Jobs, But It Won't Make Them Loyal." *Quartz at Work*. Published May 15. https://qz.com/work/1276917/money-will-attract-millennials-to-jobs-but-it-wont-make-them-loyal/.

Covey, S. R. 1999. *Principle-Centered Leadership*. New York: Simon & Schuster.

Durbin, D.-A. 2006. "Ford Takes Close Look at Itself as Job, Factory Cuts Are Set." *Arizona Daily Star*, January 24.

Gayle, L. 2019. "How Generation Z Is Transforming the Workplace," *Financial Executives International*. Published August 22. www.financialexecutives.org/FEI-Daily/August-2019/How-Generation-Z-Is-Transforming-the-Workplace.aspx.

Inspiration Office. 2018. "6 Ways to Make the Workplace More Age-Neutral." TimesLIVE (South Africa). Published May 21. www.timeslive.co.za/sebenza-live/features/2018-05-21-6-ways-on-how-to-make-the-workplace-more-age-neutral/.

McGregor, L., and N. Doshi. 2015. "How Company Culture Shapes Employee Motivation." *Harvard Business Review*. Published November 25. https://hbr.org/2015/11/how-company-culture-shapes-employee-motivation.

Peters, K., and A. Haslem. 2018. "Research: To Be a Good Leader, Start by Being a Good Follower." *Harvard Business Review*. Published August 6. https://hbr.org/2018/08/research-to-be-a-good-leader-start-by-being-a-good-follower.

Schwantes, M. 2020. "How Can You Tell You Work for a Toxic Boss? They're Known for These 5 Things." *Inc.* Published September 3. www.inc.com/marcel-schwantes/toxic-boss-signs.html.

Senge, P. M. 2010. *The Fifth Discipline: The Art and Practice of the Learning Organization*. New York: Doubleday.

Shein, E. 2021. "Report: Generation Z and Millennials Have Different Expectations Around Tech Preferences." TechRepublic. Published March 16. www.techrepublic.com/article/report-generation-z-and-millennials-have-different-expectations-around-tech-preferences/.

Society for Human Resource Management (SHRM). 2020. "Engaging Remote Workers." *Daily Newsletter*. Published spring. www.shrm.org/resourcesandtools/tools-and-samples/exreq/pages/details.aspx?erid=1447.

———. 2017. *SHRM Customized Talent Acquisition Benchmarking Report*. Published December. www.shrm.org/hr-today/trends-and-forecasting/research-and-surveys/Documents/2017-Talent-Acquisition-Benchmarking.pdf.

Vozza, S. 2020. "How to Spot a Potentially Toxic Hire During a Job Interview." *Fast Company*. Published October 22. www.fastcompany.com/90566299/how-to-spot-a-toxic-person-during-a-job-interview.

CHAPTER 6

Leadership Behaviors That Drive Engagement

The challenge of leadership is to be strong but not rude; be kind, but not weak; be bold, but not a bully; be humble, but not timid; be proud, but not arrogant; have humor, but without folly.

—Jim Rohn

THE CHALLENGE OF effective leadership begins with individual leader behavior. More than your intellect, technical skills, talent, personality, processes, or strategy, individual leader behavior is the single most important predictor of an organization's performance. The primary success of leaders depends on their ability to match their behavior to unpredictable and changing situations. Context matters and contextual variables create challenges for how a leader deploys strategy, makes decisions, manages processes, and uses technical skills. Context and contextual variables also create challenges for how a leader needs to use behavioral skills.

The ability of leaders to remain flexible in their behavior no matter the situation and context is the key variable in promoting and sustaining employee engagement to drive performance. Leading from your upper brain means managing behavior effectively in response to the stress created by changing context. Doing so allows you to connect to and engage your technical skills to function at optimal levels of performance.

THE MAKING OF EFFECTIVE LEADERS

We know that a leader's ability to manage context is a critical factor for evaluating leadership effectiveness. Consequently, to achieve organizational performance, either the organization needs to adapt by matching different leaders to different contexts, or leaders need to adapt by matching their behaviors to different contexts. The fundamental question we seek to answer is this: What kind of leader should organizations search for to create engagement and get results in these increasingly complex, chaotic, and uncertain times?

Contingency theories exist to try to explain why leadership effectiveness depends on the former approach—matching different leader traits (including gender) to the context or situation. We will discuss some of these contingency models before presenting our behavior-based solution for creating effective leaders: We believe that effective leadership is the product of adaptable leaders learning to match their behaviors to the context, *apart* from other traits those leaders might possess.

There is much debate about the key elements that make an effective leader. All the approaches discussed in this chapter are theoretical. Some have more scientific support than others, and scholars do not always agree on the criteria for effective leadership. This much is certain: Any company or organization that fails to invest in the development of its people, particularly its leaders, will always underperform organizations that do.

We will begin by dispelling five fundamental myths of effective leadership:

1.   Leaders are born, not made; leadership is a collection of innate traits that cannot be taught.
2.   Leadership is the action of an individual genius—the proverbial rock star often at the top of the organizational chart.
3.   Leaders must be charismatic extroverts to inspire and motivate their team members to connect to vision and engage in their work.
4.   Leadership requires formal authority, title, and power.
5.   A common set of traits defines all effective leaders.

Despite decades of research and study in leadership, none of these leadership myths has any scientific support. We believe that effective leadership is about transforming people and leading their upper brains to higher levels of performance outcomes. John Kotter laid the foundation for this line of reasoning more than a decade ago when he promoted the following three fundamental processes of effective leadership (Kotter and Heskett 2011):

1.   Establishing a compelling vision and strategies for achieving it.
2.   Aligning people by communicating the vision, building shared understanding, and influencing people to believe in the vision.
3.   Motivating people to work to achieve the vision.

Within this framework, we begin our discussion of contingency theory and some of the key related theories. We will demonstrate that modern, knowledge-oriented organizations require a new way of thinking about leadership development and new standards for evaluating leadership effectiveness.

Contingency Theories of Leadership

In any major field of study, there are a variety of theories that seek to provide meaning and understanding to phenomena associated with that field. Leadership is no exception. The four main theories under the general contingency theory grouping are: (1) Fiedler's contingency theory, (2) the situational leadership theory, (3) the path–goal theory, and (4) the decision-making theory. These theories share similarities, but there are some significant differences.

Fred Fiedler (1967) posited one of the first contingency models of leadership. Fiedler's contingency theory proposes that effective leadership hinges not only on the leader's style but also on the leader's control over the situation. This theory only applies to closely supervised groups that are not team-based. According to Fiedler's theory, disposition is the main trait that defines leadership capability. Research accumulated over the years does not tend to support this approach (Landy 1989).

Ten years after Fiedler, Paul Hersey and Ken Blanchard (1977) devised what many people know informally as the Hersey-Blanchard model or the situational leadership model. Unlike other leadership theories, the Hersey-Blanchard model rejects the idea that corporations require a single approach to leadership. Instead, the model proposes a leadership style that adapts to the unique circumstances of each workplace. The success of these styles depends, in part, on the employee's job maturity (high skill versus low skill) and psychological maturity (high motivation versus low motivation). The situational leadership model is popular, but it is difficult to apply in the real world, especially in groups with widely varying skills and experience. Most importantly, the empirical support for this model and its propositions is weak.

Path–goal theory combines two popular leadership theories, goal-setting theory and expectancy theory, to propose that effective leaders help their direct-report team members attain their work goals. Under path–goal theory, leaders are responsible for ensuring that their subordinates are equipped to achieve their assigned goals.

The decision-making theory of leadership posits that effective leaders assess situations and then determine how much support the group will give toward the effort, adjusting to a participative leadership style. Three decades of research have altered the original decision-making model considerably. The fundamental problem with this theory is that its assumptions are all derived from a twentieth-century perspective of the relationship between leaders and followers. It requires significant refinement to have any relevance for leaders in the twenty-first century, who face the challenges of a global economy, an increasingly technological evolution of the workplace, contributions of group effort instead of individual effort, and nontraditional employment conditions.

The main premise of all these contingency theories of leadership is that the style of leadership is what affects success or failure in a given situation. In any situation, the task, the leader's personality traits, and the personality traits shared among team members determine whether a particular leadership style will be effective. In other words, the basic assumption of these theories is that leadership success or failure is situational (Binney 2018).

Leadership Styles

Advocates for contingency theory approaches typically identify an individual's leadership style using personality-based assessment tools and then assign leadership roles or tasks based on the results. For example, the visioning process is supposed to be natural for someone with a dominant, task-oriented leadership style, but harder for a person who has a supportive, people-oriented leadership style. A supportive style is supposedly better suited to encouraging collaboration, while someone with a dominant style supposedly struggles at this.

Proponents of this type of model encourage leaders to embrace their primary style but also to step out of their comfort zone and exhibit some of the other leadership traits when necessary. The major problem with that approach is that stepping out of your personality's comfort zone is extremely difficult and requires a lot of effort and energy. Ask any introvert to behave like an extrovert and observe their reaction. This kind of flexing is stressful and negatively affects other aspects of the person's performance.

Many industrial and organizational psychology professionals are captivated by personality-based approaches to leadership development. Human resources professionals have historically used personality testing as part of their recruitment and promotion processes despite challenges from psychologists asserting that such tests are not valid predictors of job performance. Researcher Neal W. Schmitt put it more bluntly when discussing a joint paper: "Why are we looking at personality as a valid predictor of job performance when the validities haven't changed in the past twenty years and are still close to zero?" (Amble 2007). *The Cult of Personality Testing,* by Annie Murphy Paul (2005), reveals the flaws of personality assessments in terms of poor interpretation of the results, but also their poor use of the scientific method and the lack of reliability and validity of these tools.

One driver behind these testing models is an effort to determine what it takes to alter a person's personality, or even whether it is possible. The Personality Change Consortium, led by Wiebke Bleidorn and Christopher Hopwood of the University of California, Davis (2019), found evidence in one research review that "personality traits can change through persistent intervention and major life events" but that such changes would be difficult. Behavior changes, by comparison, are much easier.

We take up this debate between personality and behavior in greater detail in part III, because it is vitally important to your leadership development strategy. Suffice it to say here that the research is clear—personality is a poor predictor of performance. Your personality is who you are; your behavior is what you do.

Consequently, your leadership effectiveness is a matter of aligning your behavior with the specific requirements of your job and the constant shifts of contextual variables. Creating and maintaining this alignment requires you to lead with your upper brain.

Collaboration

Leadership, at its core, is about getting a group of people to accomplish something that one person cannot do alone. Effective leadership is about inspiring others to achieve performance excellence to accomplish mutually beneficial and meaningful objectives. Effective leaders rely on collaboration and trust the collective intelligence and talent of their teams, knowing that people, not processes, strengthen or weaken the organization's pursuit of continuous performance excellence.

Effective leaders succeed by relying on behaviors that create trust, compassion, safety, and hope among other leaders and team members. They act with integrity, authenticity, and personal accountability. This effective leadership persona creates powerful collaborations to achieve performance results and drive continuous performance improvement.

A true collaboration is characterized by effective communication, cooperative attitudes, and integrated teams; these traits distinguish a collaborative team from a group of people assigned to complete technical tasks. These behaviors are evident in the science-based characteristics of high-performing teams. Behavioral attributes (including interpersonal relationship skills) that are commonly and incorrectly called soft skills are really the hard skills that enable the leader to be effective—self-aware, self-managed, collaborative, and connected.

Low employee motivation, high burnout rates, refusal to engage in work, mistrust of management, and poor technical performance can all result when a leader consistently displays negative, disruptive, toxic behavior. Your leadership obligation is to create a culture of well-being and performance excellence where your people discover personal joy in their work and provide you, their leader, with extraordinary results. Ultimately, your leadership effectiveness in creating engagement and driving performance results to their highest levels requires you to build high-performing teams. You cannot succeed as a leader without them.

BUILDING TRUST

Real teamwork revolves around shared purpose. Trust allows your team members to adopt a shared purpose. By now, you should recognize the cause-and-effect relationships involved in effective leadership behavior. Here is a brief reminder of the discussion on trust in chapter 4:

1. Connecting with people by understanding who they are and how they experience their roles builds trust.
2. Your employees will look for evidence of your personal character and technical competence to build trust.
3. You build trust by consistently being genuine and authentic, day in and day out.

People will only connect to shared purpose, engage in their work, and create high-performing teams that drive performance outcomes when they have the necessary level of trust. To create that level of trust you must learn and practice seven fundamental leader behaviors.

Attentiveness

Effective leaders are present and responsive to the needs of their team members. They give their key people their undivided attention every day. Whether using leader huddles, the old Hewlett-Packard "leading by wandering around" approach, or rounding for outcomes, leadership connection begins by being available and genuinely attentive to the needs of the people doing the work of the organization. Do not convey, "Here I am. What do you want to tell me?" Nothing will more clearly signal a negative attitude than impatient comments directed at your team members. Isolate yourself as a leader, at any level, and you do so at your own risk and to the peril of your organization's performance.

Alertness

Effective leaders have a highly developed empathic sense. They can tell when another person is in emotional distress and respond to what they see. The most effective leaders use this ability to discern whether a team member is using their upper or lower brain.

More attitudes are communicated through facial expressions than most people realize. A person's forehead, eyes, and mouth will often reveal when their inner emotional state is in conflict with their words and behavior. Unfortunately, leaders too often dismiss the value of a person's facial expressions because they feel that the other person is "too emotional" or is challenging their authority. Failing to be alert and responsive to people's emotions is a major impediment to strategy execution.

When you are talking about controversial subjects, watch someone's eyes and mouth if you want to discern their preferences or state of mind. Be willing to change your behavior or change the words you are using if you see a negative reaction to them. Record in your mental library the words and actions that cause negative reactions so you can avoid them in the future.

Appreciation

Effective leaders are constantly looking for opportunities to praise people, and they share that praise daily. Leaders are too often critically minded and quick to verbalize other people's faults. There is a leadership myth that it is the leader's responsibility to catch people doing things wrong, but the opposite is true—leaders should spend a great deal of time catching people doing the right things and acknowledging them for it.

Not only is it hard for some leaders to look for things to praise, but when they do see something positive, these leaders also tend to take the good for granted and fail to express their appreciation for the great work. You know how you respond to positive encouragement in your own work. Well, so do the people who work for you. Everyone enjoys receiving expressions of appreciation, regardless of their position on an organizational chart.

Expressing appreciation is good for both the giver and the receiver. Appreciation fosters a positive attitude and work ethic. Learn to be an encourager of others, express your appreciation for their good work, and watch their engagement and execution of your plan drive performance.

Thoughtfulness

Any successful leader knows that effective communication is critical to execution and peak performance. Do you make decisions independently, or do you include your team members in the decision-making process? Are you open to suggestions? Do you express thoughtfulness as a form of inclusive, participative leadership in your daily relationships with your team members?

Autocratic, independent behavior in a leader breeds contempt and, in the worst case, leads to open rebellion in the workplace. A thoughtful leader will always solicit feedback from those being most affected by a decision, especially regarding potentially far-reaching consequences not immediately apparent in a high-level overview.

Do not be surprised if it takes some time to coax your team members to provide their input and to believe that you are sincere in seeking their opinions and ideas. It may take some time to build trust if it is currently absent, but it is worth the time and effort. When we display kindness and thoughtfulness—for example, by acts of acknowledgment and inclusion—our brains release oxytocin, a hormone that promotes social bonding, along with serotonin and dopamine, compounds that relieve pain, depression, and anxiety. This hormonal action in our brains creates a kindness feedback loop by prompting feelings of warmth, trust, safety, and belonging. Habitual thoughtfulness builds positive emotional connections between leaders and their employees—connections that are essential to execution and peak performance. This improved performance will be proof of your leadership effectiveness.

Dedication to Improvement

Success in every aspect of life is directly related to your ability and willingness to learn, adapt, and grow. Dan Sullivan and Catherine Nomura put it well in *Laws of Lifetime Growth* (2016, 2): Growth is a fundamental human need, "at the root of everything that gives us a feeling of accomplishment, satisfaction, meaning," and purpose in life. You may recall that we emphasized the need for effective leaders to commit to lifelong learning in the introduction to this book. Great relationships, by their nature, require constant tending. The quality of the care you put into relationships translates into either a positive or negative experience of your behavior in the lives of other people.

When leaders share meaningful learning experiences with their employees, the levels of employee engagement and leader support naturally go up. When employees have leaders who are invested in their success, meet their legitimate needs, and acknowledge their hard work, those employees try harder not only to meet but also to exceed technical and behavioral performance expectations. Investing in continuous learning changes the people and the organization—a constant evolution in our thoughts and actions in response to new understanding, new knowledge, and new skills. A closed-minded, negative attitude toward continuous improvement can destroy any chance for learning, and when there is no learning, there is no growth.

Humility

There is a powerful connection between humility and leadership influence. "Only a small percentage of people are continually successful over the long run. These outstanding few recognize that every success comes through the assistance of many other people—and they are continually grateful for this support" (Sullivan and Nomura 2016). You cannot be a successful leader unless you have support from others who are willing to contribute to your success and the success of the organization. No one wins alone, regardless of their individual talent.

Jim Collins identified humility as a key leadership characteristic in *Good to Great* decades ago, and humility remains the topic of current articles (Bourke and Titus 2020). Collins and his team pointed out "the window and the mirror": the greatest leaders tend to look in the mirror to find the source of errors or mistakes when things go wrong, and to look out the window to acknowledge employees or good fortune when things go well.

As a leader, can you give up your "right" to find fault with others and accept personal accountability and responsibility for your stewardship obligation? Can you be open to receiving candid feedback about your own behavior and its impact on those you lead? Can you get excited about letting others help you learn about your own behaviors so you can improve your leadership effectiveness? Much is written these days about the lack of employee engagement, motivation, and performance. Is it possible that this perceived lack is merely a reflection of ineffective leadership? Unless you learn to lead with humility, you will not even be willing to ask the questions.

Selflessness

The highest state of human development is demonstrated when a person consistently places the needs of others ahead of their own. These rare individuals have a mindset of others before self. The leadership literature calls people who aspire to and attain this level of selflessness *servant leaders*.

A selfless servant leader focuses on other people. Effective leaders view their key role as supporting and serving their employees as they grow and learn. These leaders cultivate an atmosphere of continuous learning and encourage their employees by seeking out ideas and praising their achievements. Such leadership behavior is the key to high employee engagement, helping people feel purposeful, motivated, and energized, so they come to work to focus on and further the goals and objectives of the organization. Selfless, other-oriented behavior demonstrates that the leader is there for team members when they most need support. Are you available to your team when they need you most?

THE SECRET SAUCE OF HIGH-PERFORMING TEAMS

We do not know of any organization that does not have a set of defined core values. We do find many organizations, such as Enron, where leaders did not connect their core values of integrity, communication, respect, and excellence to their core business practices. As a result, these values were merely empty platitudes hanging in decorative frames on walls throughout the organization.

There is a direct relationship between the ethical climate of an organization and the ethical behavior of leaders and their team members (Wimbush, Shepard, and Markham 1997). An organization that has designed and fostered an ethical climate and culture should be less likely to tolerate unethical and toxic behaviors by its members—leaders included. The values and behaviors of senior leadership especially influence the culture of the organization, and ultimately the behavior performance of their team members. Leadership behavior is the major factor in the formation of high-performing teams.

A high-performing team is more than just a group of people who are required to work together. At its core, the formation of a high-performing team begins with a shared purpose and common goal. The ability to get along—the focus of most team-building exercises—is important, but it only has value when it helps people get the job done. Ultimately, the purpose of the team is to perform, produce results, and advance the goals and objectives of the organization. An effective leader's primary responsibility is to generate the team unity and shared purpose that creates engagement and produces results at the highest sustainable levels.

You can find a host of leadership resources on the common attributes that make up an engaged and high-performing team. Following are the most frequently cited elements.

- *Trust.* A high-performing team has high levels of trust among its members. They respect each other and value what each member brings to the team. They also respect and value differences in thoughts and experiences.

- *Purpose.* When team members share a common purpose, they are willing to subordinate self-interest for the sake of the team. Accordingly, this shared sense of purpose ensures the team is pulling together, staying aligned with objectives and key results, and moving in the same direction to drive performance. When there is clarity of purpose, everyone can be engaged and committed to achieving the desired results.

- *Accountability.* A high-performing team not only talks about the importance of accountability, but they also hold each other accountable to the desired business results. Accountability also prompts the team to look for continuous performance improvement opportunities. If a process or procedure is not working, then they look for a better way.

- *Inclusivity.* A high-performing team understands that inclusion taps into the collective intelligence of a team. It allows for multiple perspectives in problem-solving and ensures that every team member has the opportunity to participate, contribute, and celebrate the overall achievements of the team. Accommodating a variety of behaviors, strengths, and preferences enriches the team's results.

- *Learning.* Even the best teams have opportunities to improve. High-performing teams actively look for those opportunities. The team members encourage feedback and use it to learn and grow, constantly striving for higher levels of performance.

- *Celebrating.* Celebrating creates positive emotional connections to the work of a high-performing team. Group celebrations and acknowledgments encourage team members to drive performance on their next project so they can win again. Nothing feeds the hunger for growth and achievement more than the experience of being a winner.

- *Communication.* High-performing teams manage confrontation and conflict in healthy ways. They have clear expectations and commit to honesty, eliminating toxic behaviors such as gossip, negativity, and office politics that obstruct performance.

- *Shared leadership.* The leader of a high-performing team is always someone who does not rely on formal authority. These leaders are willing to defer to members of the team and use collaborative, adaptive leadership practices when appropriate. The effective leader of a high-performing team always accepts full responsibility for the team's results but will delegate authority, share the problem-solving and decision-making process, and most importantly, create opportunities for the collective talent, intellect, and skill of all team members to drive results.

High-performing teams drive the performance of an organization. They do not happen by accident. Leaders need to be intentional about creating the level of engagement that produces a high-performing team, by ensuring their own highly effective leadership behavior.

ENGAGEMENT AND LEADERSHIP EFFECTIVENESS

We started this chapter by proposing that the primary success of leaders depends on their ability to match their behavior to unpredictable and changing situations. Context matters, and contextual variables create challenges for how a leader deploys strategy, makes decisions, manages processes, and uses their technical skills and behavior skills effectively. A leader's ability to remain flexible in their behavior no matter the situation is the key variable in promoting and sustaining employee engagement to drive performance. Leading from your upper brain means managing behavior effectively in response to the stress created by changing contexts. Doing so allows you to engage your technical skills to function at optimal levels of performance.

What you have discovered to this point is that self-awareness and self-management of behavior are the key elements of an effective leader. When you can regulate your thoughts and emotions—leading yourself with your upper brain—you develop the capacity to lead the brains of your team members to higher levels of engagement as well. Engagement then becomes the byproduct of effective leadership and organizational culture. When team members do not function as a high-performing team and display disengaged performance behaviors, thereby producing poor results, it is easy to blame the lack of resources, ineffective processes, or disruptive contextual variables. More often than not, however, disengagement boils down to a lack of effective leadership and a toxic organizational culture. We will investigate the aspects of organizational culture and its role in creating engagement in the next chapter.

KEY TAKEAWAYS

- The primary success of leaders depends on their ability to match their behavior to unpredictable and changing situations.
- Any company or organization that fails to invest in the development of its people, particularly its leaders, will always underperform organizations that do.
- Personality is a poor indicator and predictor of performance.
- Your leadership obligation is to create a culture of well-being and performance excellence, where your people discover personal joy in their work and provide you, their leader, with extraordinary results.
- An organization that has designed and fostered an ethical climate and culture should be less likely to tolerate unethical and toxic behaviors by its members—leaders included.

PUT IT TO WORK

1. What's the best team-building event you have ever tried? The worst? How did the event help or hinder your team? What would your ideal team-building event look like?
2. How do you currently measure the performance of your team? Does each member of your team have a personal performance development plan that focuses

on key behavior changes to improve effectiveness and performance? Do you?

3. What core values have you and your team developed that connect you and help you maintain alignment with your primary objectives and key results?

4. Do your team members know how to support each other in achieving shared objectives and desired outcomes? Create a set of promises that each member of your team can support, describing the necessary behaviors.

5. What is the current level of trust on your team? How do you know and how would you measure it? What do you need to do to improve the level of trust on your team?

6. What level of accountability exists within your team and your organization? To assess this, consider the following questions:

    - What are the tangible and intangible costs of toxic behavior?

    - What behavioral and performance expectations or standards are in place for the team and for the organization as a whole?

    - Does anyone consistently display poor behavior that affects the functioning of the team? What have you done to confront this behavior? Has your response been effective? Why or why not?

    - How do you deal with disruptive behaviors? How do your team members handle disruptive behaviors within their own groups?

REFERENCES

Amble, B. 2007. "Personality Tests Poor Predictors of Job Performance." *Management Issues*. Published December 13. www.management-issues.com/news/4687/personality-tests-poor-predictors-of-job-performance/.

Binney, E. 2018. "What Type of Leader Are You?" Society for Human Resource Management. Published October 5. www.shrm.org/resourcesandtools/hr-topics/organizational-and-employee-development/pages/what-type-of-leader-are-you.aspx.

Bourke, J., and A. Titus. 2020. "The Key to Inclusive Leadership." *Harvard Business Review*. Published March 6. https://hbr.org/2020/03/the-key-to-inclusive-leadership.

Fiedler, F. 1967. *A Theory of Leadership Effectiveness*. New York: McGraw-Hill.

Hersey, P., and K. H. Blanchard. 1977. *Management of Organizational Behavior: Utilizing Human Resources*, 3rd ed. Englewood Cliffs, NJ: Prentice Hall.

Kotter, J. P., and J. L. Heskett. 2011. *Corporate Culture and Performance*. New York: Free Press.

Landy, F. 1989. *Psychology of Work Behavior*. Pacific Grove, CA: Brooks/Cole.

Paul, A. M. 2005. *The Cult of Personality Testing: How Personality Tests Are Leading Us to Miseducate Our Children, Mismanage Our Companies, and Misunderstand Ourselves*. New York: Free Press.

Sullivan, D., and C. Nomura. 2016. *The Laws of Lifetime Growth: Always Make Your Future Bigger Than Your Past*, 2nd ed. Oakland, CA: Berrett-Koehler Publishers.

University of California, Davis. 2019. "Scientists Say You Can Change Your Personality: But It Takes Persistent Intervention." *ScienceDaily*. www.sciencedaily.com/releases/2019/12/191212142659.htm.

Wimbush, J., J. Shepard, and S. Markham. 1997. "An Empirical Examination of the Relationship Between Ethical Climate and Ethical Behavior from Multiple Levels of Analysis." *Journal of Business Ethics* 16 (16): 1705–16.

PART III

Performance

Leadership is a potent combination of strategy and character. But if you must be without one, be without the strategy.

—attributed to Norman Schwarzkopf Jr.

CONTINUOUS PERFORMANCE IMPROVEMENT is no longer an organizational luxury; it is a sustainability imperative. Continuous performance improvement requires leaders to understand change management and human behavior. Change and performance improvement are no longer on the periphery but rather require leaders' daily focus. Leaders struggle with both the process and behavior dimensions of performance as they relate directly to continuous performance improvement. Implementation challenges on Lean and Six Sigma projects or when installing electronic health record systems bear witness to this fact. The fundamental problem for leaders is figuring out how to align the science of continuous improvement with the neuroscience of human behavior. Management of the contextual variables between process and people is essential to promoting the fundamental performance behaviors that produce actual results. The solution to this problem is not found in either/or approaches to performance, but in using a combination of technical and behavioral capacities.

The fundamental responsibility of leaders is producing results—achieving the strategic goals and objectives that define the organization's purpose. We all are familiar with the lists of leadership competencies and disciplines needed to get results: vision, strategy, marketing, innovation, agility, execution, and more. We can think of all these things as the core components of business management. But as necessary as they might be for any organization to produce results, organizational management components do not get things done—people do. Leaders do not lead marketing plans and business development models; they lead people. Without the efforts of highly engaged people, nothing gets done. Richard Branson and other inspiring leaders affirm the importance of putting employees first to get results.

For nearly a decade, neuroscience and performance experts have been teaming up to produce research demonstrating that the biggest opportunity for competitive advantage arises from people making mental and emotional connections with their leaders. We now have ample evidence demonstrating that engagement drives employee performance, and organizational results are the sum of the performance of all employees. The consistent value of those results to the customers, clients, and patients on the receiving end determines the success and long-term viability of the organization.

Ironically, despite the growing evidence connecting behavior and performance, senior leaders have expressed little interest in focusing on behavior capacity, preferring to continue their efforts to optimize process capacity. Consequently, most leaders get minimal skill, talent, and intellect from their team members, thereby yielding only nominal performance to create results of value. By learning and applying the key elements of performance behavior, shrewd leaders can fully tap into the skill, talent, and intellect of their team members. As we learned in part II, these engaged team members drive performance to the highest levels, ensuring the organization's long-term growth and sustainability.

The current focus on process capacity is based on outdated science and does not meet the challenges of hiring and developing knowledge-based workers in the twenty-first century—and executives know this. In one survey by Deloitte (2015), 58 percent of executives believed that their current performance management approach drove neither employee engagement nor high performance. Accordingly, we are offering you an opportunity to redesign the key elements of your performance management system.

Our approach requires leaders to attend to behavior development first. The development of *behavior capacity*—the observable and measurable actions of a person or group of people—must align with *process capacity*—the sum of the efforts of everyone in the organization to know and connect to the organization's strategic objectives and key results—in order to drive performance to the highest levels. When we know which behaviors are necessary to achieve performance and we align those behaviors to the processes required to do the work, the outcomes are results of lasting value.

Understanding and managing the relationship between process capacity and behavior capacity is essential for leaders who want to create and sustain high levels of performance outcomes. Performance then becomes an observable and measurable function of the desired results and the behavior required to produce those results. Leaders can train and coach their team members in those behaviors to produce the results the leader desires.

By applying the science of appropriate behaviors that align with the science of technical processes, you will build a performance architecture designed to achieve a predictable set of outcomes. You can learn and implement a systematic approach to developing the process and behavior capacities that will produce the outcomes and results you desire. In the next three chapters we will explore the nature of organizational performance and its functional relationship to the technical and behavioral skill capacities necessary to create it.

Chapter 7, "The Performance Equation," redefines the key element of performance as behavior capacity, not technical skill, talent, or intellect. A universal and eternal truth in the life cycle of high-performance organizations is that individual breakthroughs drive organizational breakthroughs. Reducing the variability of leadership effectiveness is critical to achieving the overall objective of organizational performance excellence. Consistently effective leadership, then, is a means to a greater end, particularly in healthcare—safer practices, higher quality care measures, and patient care experiences that create high levels of service satisfaction.

Chapter 8, "The Technical Tyrant," explains why performance is not defined merely by technical skills, processes, and strategic plans. Typically, leadership failure is not the result of poor technical skills but of poor behavioral skills. You may gain higher levels of management responsibility based on your technical skills, but your overall leadership effectiveness is clearly dependent on your behavior skills. The truth is that the so-called soft skills of behavior are really the hard skills that create leadership effectiveness. Time and again, the fundamental problems of poor engagement and poor work performance stem from how people experience their leaders' negative behaviors, not from their leaders' lack of technical competence.

Finally, in chapter 9, "Behavior Capacity," we show you how to leverage performance behavior to drive technical skills to their highest level of performance potential. We explore the science behind recruiting and developing top talent and then engaging that talent to drive results to the highest level.

Every organization around the world is competing to find and cultivate effective leaders. Surveys of senior leaders have consistently indicated a fear of not having enough emerging leaders to guide their organizations through the significant challenges of the twenty-first century, even before the COVID-19 pandemic. We are convinced that our method provides an easy-to-use model for becoming an effective leader. You can use this model every day to confront and overcome your most significant leadership challenges.

KEY TAKEAWAYS

- Leaders do not lead marketing plans and business development models; they lead people. Without the efforts of highly engaged people, nothing gets done.
- Leaders now have evidence linking business performance to a fundamental understanding of what creates employee engagement and drives performance.
- Understanding and managing the relationship between process capacity and behavior capacity is essential for leaders who want to create and sustain high levels of performance outcomes.

REFERENCE

Deloitte. 2015. *Global Human Capital Trends 2015: Leading in the New World of Work*. New York: Deloitte University Press.

CHAPTER 7

The Performance Equation

We are what we repeatedly do. Excellence, then, is not an act,
but a habit.

—attributed to Aristotle

IN THIS CHAPTER we introduce you to the performance equation. The performance equation is the function of technical capacity and behavior capacity:

Performance = $f(x)$ (technical capacity) × (behavior capacity)

As mentioned previously, what has typically been missing from books on performance and leadership is a single model or system that combines the essentials of effective leadership and high performance in an integrated performance management framework or architecture. In chapter 1, we introduced you to the effective leadership equation. We started building our performance management system with effective leadership because effective leadership is everything. As Henry Cloud (2013) would say, "Leadership matters when it comes to creating results. It matters for the entire organization, and it matters for departments and teams."

Then we discovered another performance dimension in chapter 4—namely, engagement. Engagement is the engine that drives behavior capacity (discussed in chapter 9). Engagement is the willingness to focus on and execute the key objectives and performance indicators of the organization at the highest levels. We emphasized in previous chapters that engagement is not a personality trait; it is a behavior choice. Performance is determined by your behavior (what you do), not your personality (who you are).

It is absolutely critical not to confuse behavior and personality in relationship to performance. Regardless of your personality type, performance always results from your behavior. Your behavior is the byproduct of your thoughts and emotions as you process stimuli from your external environment—your daily life experiences. Research shows that our brain, just like our senses, reacts best to constantly changing stimuli (Leaf 2013). As we consciously direct our thinking, we can be purposeful in exhibiting behaviors that most effectively produce results of value.

On that note, we can now shift our focus to the final equation of our behavior-based performance management system. To get results at a high level and make a difference in performance outcomes, leaders need to understand the undeniable link between process capacity and behavior capacity. Ignoring the science of behavior and its impact on process, skill, talent, intellect, critical thinking, and strategic planning—upper-level brain functions—jeopardizes an organization's ability to sustain continuous performance improvement.

Effective leadership is essential to performance because you cannot achieve a high level of engagement from team members who lack effective leadership connections. Engagement is essential to performance because you cannot achieve a high level of behavior capacity (executive upper-brain function) from people who lack engagement.

When people cannot connect to and activate their prefrontal cortex, the performance part of their brain (behavior capacity), they cannot connect to their skill, talent, and intellect (process capacity) to execute on strategy and produce results of value at a high level (performance). The process capacity coefficient of this equation is the dependent variable. It depends on the level of behavior capacity to maximize performance outcomes. This is why everything we teach about leadership and performance depends on this solitary premise: Individual leader behavior is the single most important predictor of how individuals and teams perform to produce results.

Unless people can build a strong, positive emotional connection to their leader's behavior, they cannot activate the part of their brains that creates the behaviors that produce performance at a high level. It is all in the physiology of the how the brain functions—or, as we like to say, it is all in how you mix the neurochemical cocktail in people's brains. Given how profoundly a leader's behavior affects the performance response of team members, you ignore this neurochemical reality at your own performance peril. Effective leaders behave in ways that make it possible for the brains of their people to function in ways that produce results at high levels. When you display the right behaviors, people will follow you gladly and will strive for performance excellence.

Somewhere in the midst of all the *doing* of total quality and continuous improvement of processes and systems, we neglected to grasp that the very essence of process improvement is a mindset, a philosophy about providing high-quality products and excellence in service and business performance. We seem to be convinced that W. Edwards Deming was all about focusing on processes and systems and not on behavior. If something is not working well, then don't look at the people; look at the process. How many problems in safety, quality, and service do you currently face in your organization? How many failure mode and effects analysis teams and root cause analysis teams have you participated in to find solutions to these problems? Were members of these teams willing to look at human behavior as a primary cause of safety violations, poor quality in production cycles, or rude customer service?

Deming continually emphasized that organizational quality is not always a function of doing things better but sometimes of doing things differently. Doing things differently requires changing our thinking so we can, in turn, change what we believe, thereby enabling us to change how we behave. In calling for a transformation of management operations, Deming was calling for a fundamental change in leader and manager behavior. Total quality as a philosophy—and continuous performance improvement as a reality—is clear: You cannot expect organizations to change unless the people do. Individual breakthroughs drive organizational breakthroughs.

CORE COMPONENTS OF HIGH PERFORMANCE

In a competitive world, performance is everything. To get results at a high level and sustain those results over long periods of time requires both effective process capacity and effective behavior capacity (Stuart-Kotze 2006). High-level performance comes from doing the right things at the right time. Another way of identifying these two primary components of performance is to say that you need the right process and the right people behaving in the right way. Remember that behavior drives performance (chapter 6). Your behavior choices determine the performance outcomes in all areas of your life.

Behavior is how you act—the things you do and say. You control the actions you take and the decisions you make, and what you decide to do and when you decide to do it determine the level of your performance results. Life is never about what is happening to you but how you choose to respond to what is happening to you.

Environmental stimuli can affect what you decide to do and when you decide to it. Remember the key distinction between living life in your upper brain and in your lower brain: Your upper brain provides your ability to grow, develop, and achieve; your lower brain manages threat and survival responses. This dynamic— the polarity and tension between the upper brain and the lower brain—and its relationship to leader behavior were discussed in chapter 3. Are you leading with your upper brain, or are you yielding to the impulse to survive environmental stimuli and reacting with your lower brain?

Whether a behavior is effective and has a positive influence on performance is directly related to the job requirements and the ever-changing situations in which you work. You must exhibit certain behaviors to perform well in your role. When a person has difficulty activating their upper brain (prefrontal cortex) for performance, they will struggle to exhibit effective behaviors that match the demands of their job and produce the expected and required performance outcomes.

This is why leader behavior is so critical to the performance outcomes of a team. If leaders behave in ways that stimulate positive effects in the brains of their people—leading with their upper brains—then it becomes more realistic to expect employees to choose behaviors that link to their process capacity (i.e., manage their jobs effectively) and produce high-level results.

When a leader's behavior provokes a lack of trust, compassion, and safety, and the burden of work exceeds people's capacity to manage it effectively, then performance suffers. The ability to adapt your behavior to changing circumstances, particularly disruptive circumstances, lies at the heart of effective performance.

The process capacity coefficient of the performance equation has everything people need to align with their appropriate behaviors to produce results and drive performance. Process capacity includes vision, protocols, procedures, guidelines, technical manuals, business plans, strategic and tactical objectives, rules, financial strategies, and the practical application of continuous improvement performance methodology. The elements of the process capacity coefficient need to be clear and specific for all members at all levels of the organization to create team cohesion and allow everyone to focus on performance outcomes. Organizational objectives must align with elements of the process capacity coefficient. Leaders need to translate these organizational objectives from the strategy level to specific functional objectives at the operational level of the organization. This communication has both vertical and horizontal implications throughout the organization.

Vertical alignment in the organization ensures a solid connection between performance objectives and resources and processes needed to achieve those objectives. Consequently, the organization's most important objectives must be translated into actions to be performed. Key performance indicators and the ability to align objectives and key results identify how well people connect their individual actions, using the processes and resources at their disposal, to produce the results leaders desire.

Horizontal alignment in the organization ensures that all members of a team at the same hierarchical level, performing the same job requirements, do their work with as little variation as possible. Disruptive elements of performance often result from team members working on conflicting objectives or competing priorities. In our research, we often ask team members to identify the biggest impediments to their individual performance. Unclear objectives and competing priorities always rank in the top three responses.

When people lack clarity on objectives and priorities, they will come to work and do the things they think are most important from their own perspective. They will use their personal core values for perspective on how to perform in their work role. Conflicting values and competing priorities increase variations in work performance across the organization. Variation in the execution of work among people doing the same job hinders continuous performance improvement. Not only are there consequences to process capacity, but people also can lose motivation and engagement and put less effort into doing the work. A failure to link process capacity and behavior capacity (i.e., vertical and horizontal misalignment) has enormous implications for the overall performance of the organization.

MULTIPLYING BY ZERO

Any number times zero equals zero. This easy multiplication rule has great significance when we consider the coefficients of the performance equation. As previously mentioned, the process capacity of the performance equation has certain core components—for example, business strategy, clinical strategy, protocols and guidelines, and material resources such as hardware and software. These are the things people need to fulfill their specific job requirements. Since organizations can create and acquire these elements of process capacity, we consider this coefficient of the performance equation the dependent performance variable. The process capacity elements tend to remain stable and do not change quickly over time; the execution of those elements is dependent on behavior capacity.

Leadership failure rarely results from an absence of technical skill, talent, intellect, or other tangible elements of process capacity. Ineffective leadership and the resulting performance failures are consistently due to behavior capacity incompetence. You need only scan news headlines to substantiate this statement. High-profile leaders are losing their jobs and reputations over behavior issues related to harassment and unethical and illegal financial dealings almost daily. These high-profile leaders get into trouble because of their behavior skill lapses, not because they become incompetent in their skill, talent, or intellect.

You gain higher levels of management responsibility based on your individual technical skill performance. Your overall leadership effectiveness and success are clearly dependent on your behavior skills, since senior leadership achievement is strategically—rather than operationally—oriented. The truth is that the so-called behavioral soft skills are really the hard skills that lead to measurable leadership accomplishments and organizational performance. That is why performance ebbs and flows—because of the relationship between your process capacity and your behavior capacity. Regardless of your technical and process capacities, if you are deficient in your behavior capacity it will be clearly evident in the measurement of your leadership effectiveness.

Intentional and purposeful self-evaluation is indispensable to identifying and correcting leadership lapses and weaknesses in behavior; it is essential to the success of leaders and their organizations. Highly effective, influential leaders thrive on daily feedback regarding how others are experiencing their leadership behaviors. How about you? Are you the kind of leader others want to follow? Would you follow you as a leader? Consistently collecting feedback on your behavior may begin to make the difference for you in both personal and organizational performance. You cannot overcome your performance challenges alone.

THE SUBSTRUCTURE OF PERFORMANCE

To develop a purpose- and performance-driven culture, a key first step is for leaders at all levels to consider the effect of poor behavior on safety, quality, and service. Real change will never come from an annual conference or the latest management fad. It will come from within the organization when leaders are committed to a common purpose and behave in a way that inspires employees to achieve the organization's strategic aims. Sadly, and with great regularity, we see leaders and their organizations self-destruct because they failed to grasp the fundamental connection between individual leader behavior and organizational performance.

There is nothing more destructive to an organization than leaders who are out of touch with the effect their behavior has on their team members' performance. You have to remain relevant. Our world has changed—in many ways, for the better. Cultural revisions concerning how we treat traditionally disenfranchised minority groups have dramatically and positively transformed our workforces. If you haven't yet adapted to these realities as a leader and are still telling inappropriate jokes; using condescending phrases; continuing biased hiring, retention, and promotion practices; and holding on to other outdated and unacceptable behaviors, then you are heading for troubled waters.

Are you prepared to accept the personal and professional consequences of knowingly or unknowingly demeaning the inherent value of another human being? Disrespectful behavioral lapses will always reveal ineffective leader behavior. Time and time again, the inability or unwillingness to adapt to these cultural realities reveals leadership weaknesses that cause irreparable damage to team unity, team cohesion, and team performance.

What would you do if you discovered a way to turn on your brain that enabled you to be happier, to be more prosperous, and to achieve the goals you set? Following are three foundational skills every leader should practice to develop high-level behavior performance to maximize personal and professional goal achievement.

Connection

Success in every dimension of life is related to your ability to connect with others. Success is also directly related to your ability and willingness to learn, change, adapt, and grow. Relationships by their nature require constant and consistent tending. The quality of care you put into these relationships translates into either a negative or a positive behavior experience for other people. When leaders share meaningful learning experiences with their employees, they gain empathy and compassion for the people doing the work of the organization. You only need to watch one episode of *Undercover Boss* to appreciate this truth. In every episode, a senior leader has an epiphany regarding the burdens of work for frontline employees in their organization. Each leader learns the value of empathy and compassion to compel engagement, gain employee loyalty, and drive performance.

Power can corrupt the behavior of any leader at any level. Compassion is the antidote to the destructive nature of the power virus. The compassion and respect experienced by team members increase employee engagement (Hougaard, Carter, and Chester 2018). Undergoing a continuous learning process similar to the one experienced by the leaders in *Undercover Boss* entails change; one cannot learn and remain the same person, team, or organization. Our thoughts and actions are constantly evolving as we absorb new understanding, knowledge, and skills. When there is no learning, there is no growth.

Unity

No one wins alone, regardless of their level of individual talent. As we will see in chapter 9, certain behaviors come more naturally to certain leaders. This is clearly the case with humility, a fundamental requirement for team unity and harmony. Recall that *Good to Great* author Jim Collins (2001) deems humility a "Level 5" leadership behavior. Collins and his team discovered that Level 5 leaders always accept blame for mistakes and bestow praise for successes on others—a habit they call "the window and the mirror." In *Laws of Lifetime Growth*, Dan Sullivan and Catherine Nomura (2016) write about the connection between humility and leadership performance. They maintain that only a small percentage of people are consistently successful for long periods of time and that a leader's long-term effectiveness is predicated on receiving continual support and assistance from others. They caution isolated leaders that in the absence of unity they will lose their creativity and their ability to succeed.

As a leader, can you give up your supposed right to finding fault with others and accept personal accountability and responsibility for your stewardship obligations? Can you open yourself to receiving candid feedback about your own behavior and its impact on those you lead? Can you become excited about letting others help you learn about your own habits to improve the effectiveness of your leadership influence?

Selflessness

Effective leaders put their people first. In *High Altitude Leadership,* Chris Warner and Don Schmincke (2008, 31) discuss the debilitating toll selfishness takes on companies, calling it "dangerous, unproductive, dysfunctional behavior," or DUD behavior. Using the real-life experiences of those who have scaled the world's tallest summits, Warner and Schmincke reveal eight dangers that can not only cost you your life on a mountain but also derail your organizational strategy. Selfishness is one of these dangers.

Selfishness, or the disregard for the welfare and needs of others, will prevent you from reaching the summit of your leadership effectiveness. Selflessness, or putting the needs of others ahead of your own, is essential to creating and sustaining positive and supportive connections and unity with your team. It fuels your leadership effectiveness and drives your performance success.

THE BEHAVIOR–PERFORMANCE LINK

Significant change initiatives in organizations, especially in the wake of the COVID-19 pandemic, often focus on technology and process, neglecting to take the human factor into equal consideration. Regardless of the industry, leaders must accept that people are the most valuable asset for organizational performance. Effective leaders can manage the tensions between processes and people. They are fully aware that so-called people issues can surprise anyone, threatening the successful execution of strategy and plans.

People are not robots, and research validates that most people want meaning, value, and purpose in their work. The value shift of the twenty-first-century workforce is evidence of this. When organizations focus on aligning people with strategy and creating unity and clarity, people can drive performance to the highest levels. The healthcare industry experiences constant change in practices and in regulatory oversight, but the fundamental challenge for all leaders remains constant: How do we *lead* and *manage* (two fundamentally different executive functions) healthcare organizations despite these constant changes? The answer is effective leadership behavior.

Leadership is a behavior skill, not a technical skill. Leadership is the daily, persistent expression of behavior that positively connects with people to execute and accomplish the purpose (the why) and the mission (the what) of the organization. Effective leadership behavior creates a calm confidence that permeates any organization. We keep repeating that individual leader behavior is the single most important predictor of this high level of organizational performance because, time and again, neurophysiology continues to validate our claim. In the words of Henry Cloud (2013, 11), "When leaders lead the brains of their people the way the brain is designed to work, the people can perform at the highest levels."

Highly effective and influential leaders succeed where other leaders fail because their brains perform at a higher level. They are more productive and they achieve better results than other leaders faced with similar circumstances and given the same resources. The success and effectiveness of these leaders comes from a set of behaviors that enables them to serve as role models, guide operational improvements, consistently execute on strategy, and sustain performance excellence. In our terminology, they are leading with their upper brains. In *The Power of Neuroplasticity*, Shad Helmstetter (2013) asks us to imagine what we could do with a brain that is always clear, sharp, and alert; always thinks in the positive; deals with problems but refuses to be stopped by them; believes in your unlimited potential and inspires you to reach it; is endlessly encouraging; will do for you what you tell it to do, and is hardwired for growth, development, achievement, and success. Can you imagine what you could achieve in performance outcomes, both personally and with the collective intelligence of your team, with a brain that works as Helmstetter describes?

Highly effective and influential leaders recognize the importance of self-awareness, collaboration, and building highly effective relationships. They spend time focusing their efforts in key areas that will build connections with the people they lead to drive performance. They focus these efforts around the fundamental skill set of tactical capacity. We define *tactical capacity* as simply getting it right as a leader, both with the technical elements of performance and with people. When you have a meaningful relationship with another person, you work more effectively together. You have a common goal and a consistent purpose, your efforts are channeled toward a common outcome, and you drive performance in the organization to peak levels. For this conceptual model to work in an organization, it is essential that positive mental and neurochemical connections exist among leaders and team members throughout the entire organization.

Leaders have the responsibility to go first, demonstrating the desire for the kind of high-level relationship dynamic that fuels high-performing teams. Since leader behavior is the key to predicting team performance, we can focus on key elements of effective leadership behavior for you to practice daily with your team members:

- Accountability and transparency, including actively listening, sharing information, and taking responsibility instead of blaming.
- Genuine interest in and concern for others; empathy.
- Respectful and equal regard for and treatment of others, regardless of rank or position; inclusion.
- Focused attention.
- Principled and evidence-based decision-making.
- Dedication to keeping promises and commitments.
- Willingness to celebrate and reward good and exceptional work.
- Consistent alignment of manner, words, and actions with professed core values.

These behaviors indicate the developed self-awareness of effective leaders discussed in chapter 2. Here, these behaviors demonstrate the integrated elements of the behavior-based performance management system we recommend to leaders. As masters of interpersonal relations, effective and influential leaders know that their everyday words, actions, and habits can either strengthen or weaken relationships and have neurochemical consequences.

The limbic system of human beings can only tolerate so much bad behavior before it negatively affects relationships. The most noteworthy effect is losing the willingness to trust and beginning to feel disconnected from the leader or organization that is behaving badly. You already know the outcomes of an unmotivated, disengaged workforce, particularly in high-stress and high-risk environments. This is why, as effective leaders, we are vigilant about making decisions that foster highly effective collaborative relationships with our colleagues and team members.

Team members must trust each other for their brains to function at peak effectiveness. Trust enables the team not only to perform its daily function, but also to rise above conflicts and crises. In fact, by the strict definition of a high-performing team, if you do not have trust, then you do not have a real team. Ideally, trust should be at a high level, but at a minimum it should be at an acceptable level, allowing the team to develop and execute organizational plans and strategy. An absence of trust always has negative consequences for team unity and harmony. In addition, executives we work with say that a lack of trust damages productivity and profitability. Simply stated, low or no trust puts the organization at a competitive and performance disadvantage.

As a leader, you build or destroy trust in your organization every day. You can lead the upper brains of your people to higher levels of performance. You are uniquely responsible for your teams' results. If you have the desire, you can learn to lead from an upper brain built for performance. In doing so, you can create an amazing future for yourself and your organization.

Our goal has been to provide you with the means to create a performance architecture using an integrated, actionable conceptual model for leadership effectiveness that puts *you* back in control of leading *your* teams and *your* organization to the highest levels of performance that *you* can imagine. You are free to choose where you focus your attention, and this affects how the chemicals, proteins, and wiring of your brain change and function. Neuroscientists are proving that the relationship between what you think and how you understand yourself and the world around you—your beliefs, hopes, and thoughts—has a huge impact on how your brain works and, ultimately, the level of performance you achieve.

AN INTEGRATED APPROACH TO LEADERSHIP DEVELOPMENT

Leading researchers posit that organizations spend about $356 billion annually on training and development (Westfall 2019). Are they getting their money's worth? The evidence from some researchers is not promising (Glaveski 2019):

- 75% of 1,500 managers surveyed from across 50 organizations were dissatisfied with their company's learning and development (L&D) function;
- 70% of employees report that they don't have mastery of the skills needed to do their jobs;
- only 12% of employees apply new skills learned in L&D programs to their jobs; and
- only 25% of respondents to a recent McKinsey survey believe that training measurably improved performance.

A number of factors contribute to the failure of development programs in general and leadership development programs specifically. Among these factors is senior leadership's limited participation in the training and in holding people accountable for changing behavior. Limited participation signals a lack of commitment. The performance behavior model we have been describing throughout this book requires senior leadership to focus not only on results but also on the development of the people producing those results. Our performance equation has two key coefficients: The technical coefficient focuses on strategy, plans, and objectives, and the behavior coefficient focuses on values, competencies, and behaviors. Development programs that lack a clear connection to the key elements of performance ultimately fail to identify and define behaviors that align with objectives necessary to achieve specific results.

Another reason leadership development efforts fail is the cynicism of senior leaders. Leaders often resist investing time and money into development programs, convinced that the efforts will yield minimal benefits while requiring maximum resources. This mindset is disastrous, and it communicates to talented employees that the organization is not concerned about their growth and development. Remember, people don't quit their jobs; they quit their leaders. When an organization fails to develop its leaders (or worse, when an organization develops leaders and loses them to another organization), the impact on organizational performance is staggering.

Learning and development efforts produce minimal outcomes when learning is not integrated across the spectrum of the organization and tied to strategic goals and daily performance objectives. First, people are learning for the wrong reasons (e.g., "I need the continuing education units"). Second, they are learning the wrong things. Most leadership development programs emphasize management and financial skills (process capacity), not behavior and interpersonal skills (behavior capacity); we continue to teach about things and not about people. Third, we are learning at the wrong times. We have a massive amount of solid research that we never learned to apply. We have known for decades that "people learn best when they *have* to learn. Applying what's learned to real-world situations strengthens one's focus and determination to learn. And while psychologist Edwin Locke showed the impact of short feedback loops back in 1968 with his theory of motivation, it's still not widely practiced when it comes to corporate training" (Glaveski 2019).

The business case for more effective learning and development programs is based on the premise that effective leadership creates better business results in terms of outcomes and higher levels of performance. Current models for developing effective leaders fall short because we put too much emphasis on technical skills and process capacity and not enough on behavioral skills and leading the brains of people to higher levels of performance. The key is to maximize people's growth and development, then connect them to clearly articulated visions that translate to meaning, value, and purpose for their work.

Effective leadership behavior, or the belief that a leader's behavior is the key predictor of organizational performance, is a radical shift in leadership thinking. As we said early in this chapter, to develop a purpose- and performance-driven culture fueled by the growth and development of people, we must shift focus away from the technical elements and processes and consider the effect that poor behavior has on safety, quality, and service. This shift must start with leaders. An organization's leaders must commit to understanding the effect that being self-aware, collaborative, and connected to their followers has on performance. They must be willing to enhance their behavior competencies to unleash performance.

There is a direct relationship between performance, technical skill, and behavior skill. We will continue to elaborate on this relationship in the next two chapters. The failure to recognize, understand, and practice the elements of a performance behavior system creates performance gaps and variation in any organization. Closing the performance gap in healthcare, or any other noble enterprise, is an imperative. In the middle of this gap—between our current levels of performance and the levels we can realistically achieve—real people, the patients, are suffering real and avoidable harm. Decades of emphasis on technical skills and technical solutions have resulted in marginal improvement. The real key to improving the safety and quality of care and reducing the financial impact on a system fraught with errors and mistakes is to focus on behavioral skill development under the inspired and focused guidance of highly effective leaders.

KEY TAKEAWAYS

- For nearly a decade, neuroscience and performance experts have been teaming up to produce research demonstrating that the biggest opportunity for competitive advantage arises from people making mental and emotional connections with their leaders.

- If leaders really want to get results at a high level and make a difference in the performance outcomes of their people, then they need to understand the undeniable link between process capacity and behavior capacity. Ignoring the science of behavior and its impact on process, skill, talent, intellect, critical thinking, and strategic planning—upper-level brain functions—jeopardizes an organization's ability to sustain continuous performance improvement.

- When a leader's behavior provokes a lack of trust, compassion, and safety, and the burden of work exceeds people's capacity to manage it effectively, then performance suffers. The ability to adapt your behavior to changing circumstances, particularly disruptive circumstances, lies at the heart of effective performance.

- Your overall leadership success is dependent on your behavior skills, since senior leadership achievement is strategically—rather than operationally—oriented. The truth is that the so-called behavioral soft skills are really the hard skills that lead to measurable leadership accomplishments and organizational performance.

- Leadership is a behavior skill, not a technical skill. Leadership is the daily, persistent expression of behavior that positively connects with people to execute and accomplish the purpose (the why) and the mission (the what) of the organization.

- The business case for more effective learning and development programs is based on the premise that effective leadership creates better business results in terms of outcomes and higher levels of performance.

- To develop a purpose- and performance-driven culture, fueled by the growth and development of people, we need to shift focus away from the technical elements and processes and consider the impact that poor behavior has on safety, quality, and service.

PUT IT TO WORK

1. In your current position, do you recognize anyone as an effective leader? When this leader offers advice, why do other people listen?

   - Do you want to be around this leader to learn from more effective behaviors, actions, abilities, and effectiveness? If so, why?

   - Describe this leader's behaviors. Are they realistic about the challenges facing the organization? Are they cynical or optimistic? Do they accept responsibility for finding solutions?

2. Are there people in your organization who are fundamentally responsible for performance management? Do these roles include responsibility for continuous performance improvement? Is continuous performance improvement considered a strategic objective? Do these roles and their responsibilities have C-suite priority throughout the organization?

3. Do you have a professional development plan for your position in your organization? Do you know how to use a development plan to improve your performance? (Indeed has a good resource that will help you think through and develop key aspects of your own continuous performance improvement: www.indeed.com/career-advice/career-development/professional-development-plan. Chapter 9 will provide additional resources.)

REFERENCES

Cloud, H. 2013. *Boundaries for Leaders: Results, Relationships, and Being Ridiculously in Charge.* New York: HarperCollins.

Collins, J. 2001. *Good to Great: Why Some Companies Make the Leap and Others Don't.* New York: HarperCollins.

Glaveski, S. 2019. "Where Companies Go Wrong with Learning and Development." *Harvard Business Review.* Published October 2. https://hbr.org/2019/10/where-companies-go-wrong-with-learning-and-development.

Helmstetter, S. 2013. *The Power of Neuroplasticity.* Gulf Breeze, FL: Park Avenue Press.

Hougaard, R., J. Carter, and L. Chester. 2018. "Power Can Corrupt Leaders. Compassion Can Save Them." *Harvard Business Review.* Published February 15. https://hbr.org/2018/02/power-can-corrupt-leaders-compassion-can-save-them.

Leaf, C. 2013. *Switch On Your Brain: The Key to Peak Happiness, Thinking, and Health.* Grand Rapids, MI: Baker Books.

Stuart-Kotze, R. 2006. *Performance: The Secrets of Successful Behaviour.* London: Pearson Education Limited.

Sullivan, D., and C. Nomura. 2016. *The Laws of Lifetime Growth: Always Make Your Future Bigger Than Your Past*, 2nd ed. Oakland, CA: Berrett-Koehler Publishers.

Warner, C., and D. Schmincke. 2008. *High Altitude Leadership: What the World's Most Forbidding Peaks Teach Us About Success*. San Francisco: Jossey-Bass.

Westfall, C. 2019. "Leadership Development Is a $366 Billion Industry: Here's Why Most Programs Don't Work." *Forbes* (blog). Published June 20. www.forbes.com/sites/chriswestfall/2019/06/20/leadership-development-why-most-programs-dont-work/.

CHAPTER 8

The Technical Tyrant

We see it all the time—where the obnoxious leader rises to the top,
but we don't know much about why.

—Dayna Herbert Walker, PhD

"Is it not enough that I am good at my job?" In short, no. In 1623, John Donne wrote, "No man is an island, entire of itself." Your previous individual achievements required the assistance of others; your future achievements will also. You must accept that being good at the technical skills of your job isn't enough to make you an effective and influential leader.

Research findings by San Francisco State University Assistant Professor of Management Dayna Herbert Walker and colleagues (2020) indicate that bad bosses believe leaders should be overbearing and manipulative. They tend to justify this disruptive behavior based on their technical expertise. The reality is that performance requires both technical and behavioral skills.

We use the phrase *tyranny of the technical* to describe the mistaken belief that individual technical performance has greater value to an organization than collaborative team performance. People have a tendency to become interpersonally incompetent when they rely solely on their technical competence to define their professional success. The inability to interact well with others can stifle growth and development and lead to the creation of hostile work environments (Priesemuth 2020).

When our behavior lapses result in people withdrawing from us, we lose the opportunity for collaboration within our teams, reducing organizational performance. We must avoid depending on any one person's technical skill. Collaboration and connection are the new elements of competition and the competitive edge to performance. We must begin to trust and value the collective intelligence of team members and their ability to connect, cooperate, and work positively with others. The leader as a technical tyrant will never be able to create such high-performing teams.

Comedies often make light of dysfunctional workplaces, but real life is no comedy and workplace discontent is no joke. Before the pandemic, Gallup found that 52 percent of American workers surveyed were "in the 'not engaged' category—those who were psychologically unattached to their work and company and who put time, but not energy or passion, into their work" (Harter 2020). When a person cannot connect and cooperate with team members, their technical expertise will not be enough to advance the goals and objectives of the team.

In virtually every organization and on every team, there is one person universally regarded as detrimental to the mission, vision, and values of the enterprise. This person typically has high technical skills and no behavioral competence. These are the toxic team members, often called "the jerk at work," that everyone would fire if they had the authority to do so.

No organization needs a toxic team member. Remember, no organization can become in technical performance what its leaders and people are not in their behavior. No aspect of this scenario can be good for the overall performance of the organization and the overall well-being of the people. If you do not believe us, then conduct your own informal research: Go pick any team in your organization and ask the people on that team, one by one, who the jerk is.

We have created multiple metrics for measuring performance, but we have not created a way to measure the impact of behavioral competence; yet, without behavioral competence, there is no clear path to trust, compassion, safety, and hope. When leaders focus on strategy and process (which are obviously needed), they can forget to focus on the people doing the work. When leaders remain task- and process-focused, they can create relationship deficits that lead to employee disengagement. Disengaged employees will put in the time, but not their energy or passion.

Engaged employees who have a passion for their jobs will put as much of their hearts and souls into their activities as they can for as long as they can. We would consider these people ideal employees. When faced with a toxic work environment, a lack of connection with a leader depletes the spiritual, mental, physical, and emotional energy of even these ideal employees, damaging their morale, motivation, and performance outcomes. Things can get worse, too. This level of disengagement, extended for a long period of time, eventually leads to burnout.

In this type of environment, high performers are likely to leave the organization. Average or below-average performers fare even worse; under a task-focused leader, these employees never have a chance to learn new skills or develop their talents. Their thoughts, emotions, and behaviors get stuck in their lower brains. They come to work and spend their day surviving, not furthering the interests and objectives of the organization, never tapping into the upper-brain resources for growth, development, and higher cognitive function that drive higher levels of performance.

Over time, the poor attitudes of average or below-average performers will worsen and further poison the organizational culture of their team. In the worst-case scenario, you keep these low performers in your organization. Most of them will compel you to fire them. When you eventually get around to doing so, you have given them ample time to create a personnel profile that provides them the opportunity to take legal action against you for wrongful termination (Williams 2018).

These disruptive scenarios rarely occur in a culture where the leader is focused on both people and process. For example, the Toyota Way has two key components—the people and the process—but the emphasis is on people first.

Being focused on others means paying attention to their needs and finding out what they desire. It means minimizing or entirely avoiding negative interactions with people, treating them as equals, and sharing meaningful experiences with them. Leaders need to remember that these people do the work to accomplish goals within their organizations. As Henry Cloud would say, your people are your plan and strategy. To achieve the level of performance so many organizations desire, leaders have to be engaged with their people. This engagement process begins when the leader chooses to willingly establish powerful and positive emotional connections with the people of the organization.

INTEGRATED TEAMS

Competition is the new collaboration. Market competition is forcing an integration of effort to achieve performance. This is another reason that you can no longer rely solely on individual technical skill to attain results. An integrated team can be a powerful tool in an effective leader's performance arsenal. Improved communications and cooperative attitudes in the workplace can help you to create these integrated teams.

People are not disposable and replaceable resources. If you think of your employees as merely a means to an end, then you will not make an effort to connect with them. Remember, success is achieved by people, not by best practices and tools. The quality of your connections with people dictates the quality of the results they will achieve.

Leadership connotes guidance and forward movement. *Management*, on the other hand, implies control. Which word motivates you more? Regardless of their job title, salary, education, or skills, people have the same needs, wants, and expectations of the workplace and of other people. A management-based superiority mindset is divisive and presents a barrier to performance excellence. Integrated teams working in the conceptual understanding of collective intelligence will improve employee morale and motivation, increase productivity, and improve your organization's safety and quality outcomes.

We have heard all our lives of the importance and value of teamwork. Our teachers and coaches encouraged us to play together and understand the concept of teamwork. How do we take this long-held belief—that teamwork is more effective in driving performance—and apply it to the workplace? Is it possible to bring teamwork to an environment where our roles are viewed as independent of the goals, objectives, and mission of the organization? Yes. We create integrated teams by implementing the skill sets of improved communications and cooperative attitudes we learned long ago.

An *integrated team* is a group of people with different areas of expertise and knowledge. Members of this team function in harmony, contributing their respective technical and behavioral skills toward the completion of a task or the accomplishment of a goal. This team follows what the professional literature calls an *integrated systems approach*. In the working model of an integrated systems approach, the work is interconnected and the members are interdependent. The system can compensate for low performance in one section, lessening its impact on the system as a whole.

This is why we advocate for the adoption of the performance equation in any performance management system. Performance is a function of both technical skill and behavioral skill capacity. We aim to integrate these two skill sets rather than allow them to be antagonistic toward one another as in more traditional performance models.

The National Center for Healthcare Leadership (2019, 1) believes that "leadership drives quality healthcare and better outcomes." One of the group's key programs is Leadership Excellence Networks (LENS), which promotes integrated, collaborative projects to find solutions for critical issues facing healthcare leaders.

The work of LENS demonstrates the success of integrated team decision-making among members of this collaborative organization. LENS participants have seen improvements in organizational climate, a better understanding of organizational goals and expectations, greater individual and leader accountability, lower turnover, and higher retention of leader candidates.

There is a caveat, however. While an integrated team is optimal during an organizational crisis, crises usually bring on conflicts—including, and most significantly, conflicts caused by behavioral dysfunction among team members as demonstrated by low trust, communication lapses, lack of accountability, and competing personal agendas. Anyone can put together a working group and call it a team, but it takes an influential and effective leader to create and sustain a highly functional integrated team. Sustaining such a team requires the leader to provide guidance and structure that allows the concepts of integration and collective intelligence to flourish. For that, you will need adaptive leadership.

ADAPTIVE LEADERSHIP

As leaders, we need to focus on forming teams whose members have behavioral competencies, including interpersonal skills that enhance the team members' financial, operational, clinical, and human resources knowledge and abilities. Technical competence is necessary to achieve performance, but without behavioral competence, performance will deteriorate.

Behavioral change is essential to achieve performance, and the good news is that behavioral change is something you can control—maybe the only thing you can. As you will read in the next chapter, behavioral capacity is the independent variable that, when mixed with technical skill, the dependent variable, drives performance to the highest levels.

A leadership model that is highly compatible with the neuroscience-based leadership approach we advocate is called *adaptive leadership*. This practical leadership framework was developed by researchers at Harvard University and captured in *The Practice of Adaptive Leadership* (Heifitz, Linsky, and Grashow 2009). The key value of adaptive leadership is the practical framework it provides for individuals and organizations to engage in meaningful change at a gradual and steady pace. This methodology allows team members to manage change together over time. The elements of the framework—the focus on discovery, diagnosis, and innovative change—go hand in glove with the operational capacity of the upper brain. Your own investigation into the adaptive leadership model, its compatibility with provoking upper-brain performance, and creating a new approach to solving your critical leadership challenges will provide you with performance leverage now and into the future.

Remember that change always poses a threat to our lower brains. The threat response of the lower brain inhibits the high-level functions of the upper brain, where all your technical skills, talent, and intelligence reside, thereby disrupting performance. Consequently, any methodology, such as adaptive leadership, that helps people to maintain a calm confidence, cooperate, and collaborate together in the midst of change enhances the opportunity to continue performance at a high level.

LEADERSHIP DEVELOPMENT

Even with evidenced-based models for leadership effectiveness, the models work only to the degree that organizations have functional leadership development programs to promote them. Go online, search through a bookstore, attend another training session or seminar, and you will see that leadership is discussed everywhere. We talk about it in all aspects of life, including politics, business, and sports. People are fascinated and confounded by the concept and by the criteria for becoming a more effective leader.

In the introduction to part I, we discussed the attributes of both an ideal leader and a bad boss. Identifying the key elements of effective leadership is not difficult. The challenge is how we teach and coach leaders into more effective behaviors that manifest in effective relationships with colleagues and team members, resulting in higher performance. The fundamental purpose of the leadership programs that teach and coach these leaders should be developing behavioral skills and balancing their importance with technical skills. Yet, despite the billions of dollars spent every year on leadership development, the research shows a low return on that investment (Myers and Doyle 2020).

A number of factors contribute to the failure of leadership development programs. A critical factor that we have discovered over the years is the limited participation of senior leadership. Limited participation by senior leaders in leadership development programs signals a lack of commitment to other team members. This lack of commitment creates a lack of trust. Research by Edelman indicates that as many as one-third of employees do not trust their employer (Rowland 2016).

Recall that trust is the foundation of all effective relationships and essential for creating an engaged and committed workforce. When an organization fails to develop its leaders—or worse, when an organization develops leaders and loses them to another organization—the impact on organizational performance is staggering.

Recognizing a leader's behavior as the key predictor of organizational performance is a radical shift in leadership thinking. Developing an organizational culture that promotes the growth of both people and performance requires a change in thinking, placing equal importance on the need for technical and behavioral skills throughout the organization. This change must start with leaders at all levels. An organization whose leaders are committed to a common purpose and have the character to inspire confidence in team members is a powerful force for change in the world. Leaders who understand the impact of their individual behavior on the brains of their followers have at their disposal a new strategy for driving the performance of their organizations to new heights.

Closing the performance gap in healthcare, or any other enterprise, is an imperative. In the gap between our current levels of performance and where we can realistically improve, people are suffering real and avoidable harm. Decades of emphasis on technical skills and technical solutions have provided marginal improvement. The real key to improving safety and quality of care and reducing the financial impact of a system fraught with errors is to focus on behavioral skill development under the inspired and focused guidance of effective leaders.

HONEST FEEDBACK

Knowing what you know now from reading this book, why would you engage in an organizational practice that is guaranteed to provoke the lower brains of your team members? Yet, annual performance reviews are still commonplace. "Most employees look forward to the annual performance review the way they look forward to a root canal. Feelings range from anxiety and angst to annoyance and anger. Not that performance reviews are a thrill for managers. Typically, they involve hours of preparation, and the outcome is often an employee who is less engaged than before" (Gupta-Sunderji 2018).

The ineffectiveness of the current practice of performance evaluations comes from the tendency to focus solely on technical skills. The antiquated practice of forced ranking results in even more people who are disillusioned, disconnected, and demoralized, with lower brains that are blowing up and upper brains that are turning off. How many of you, as leaders giving these appraisals or as employees receiving them, can say that these appraisals were beneficial and effective?

Kathleen Doheny (2021), writing for the Society of Human Resource Management, discusses the transformation of large, medium, and small companies, "all eager to ditch the end-of-year performance review that can produce nail-biting anxiety for managers and workers alike, without much improvement in performance." The consensus is that the performance review process creates fear, worry, and anxiety that lasts for months. These fear responses have a significant impact on performance. So what is the alternative?

Leaders should be using tools and methodologies that promote employee growth and engagement. The objective of this growth and performance process should be helping team members find meaning and value in their work as they become successful in the performance of that work. The effective leader relates to team members as a coach, not a critic. Leaders should discover their team members' strengths, find out what they care about, and discuss their goals and dreams. Leaders need to cultivate effective relationships with team members, and to understand that these relationships require constant effort.

For example, a behavior-based performance feedback methodology that engages employees' strengths could use the following questions: Do you know what behaviors you display on a daily basis? Are your habits bringing you closer to achieving the higher levels of performance necessary to make a significant difference in the lives of others, or are they keeping you from that goal? You can also use a feedback system to solicit these comments. Here are some additional questions you can ask:

- Do you clearly communicate a vision for our team/organization?
- Do you treat people with courtesy and respect?
- Do you solicit opinions contrary to your ideas and directives?

- Do you encourage other people to share their ideas?
- Do you actively listen to other people in meetings?
- Do you give people the impression that you are accessible and approachable?

This process can and should occur not just once or twice a year, but as frequent leader-to-leader, peer-to-peer engagement sessions—every two to four weeks.

For many people, the very thought of feedback generates an immediate emotional reaction. We often do not want to hear—or we are afraid to hear—how people experience us through our behaviors. And other people often do not want to give us feedback for fear of negatively affecting the relationship. Regardless, we must recognize that giving and receiving feedback is part of developing long-lasting and productive workplace relationships—relationships that are healthy, collaborative, and built around mutual respect and trust.

Changing from stress-inducing annual reviews to frequent honest feedback sessions creates opportunities to discuss performance achievement in a constructive and positive way that will achieve sustaining results. The outdated annual review model judges only technical skill achievement and creates interoffice competition. Looking at performance reviews as a continual performance improvement process generates the type of employee engagement that produces the long-lasting performance everyone desires.

BEHAVIORAL SKILL REQUIREMENTS

Leadership failures typically do not result from an absence of technical skill, but rather from behavioral incompetence. You may gain higher levels of management responsibility based on your technical skill performance. Your overall leadership success, however, clearly depends on your behavioral skills, since senior leadership success is more strategic (behavioral skill focused) than operational (technical skill focused). As we have said previously, the so-called behavioral soft skills are really the hard skills that lead to measurable leadership effectiveness and success.

Time and again, the fundamental problems of lack of employee engagement and lack of work performance enhancement stem from people consistently experiencing their leader's negative behavior. These leadership failures can be directly linked to the three fundamental elements of influential leadership: self-awareness, collaboration, and connection. You must remember that individual leader behavior is the single most important predictor of organizational performance.

A key factor of your leadership effectiveness is discovering and developing self-awareness. Leaders need to periodically evaluate their behavior performance in light of their technical performance. The only alternative to self-evaluation is to put your behavior on autopilot. The experience of two commercial airline pilots overflying their destination by over an hour is testament to the danger of that approach—especially with something as critical to organizational success as highly effective relationships (Wald 2009).

Albert Einstein supposedly observed that problems cannot be solved with the same type of thinking that created them. We would suggest that the problems of ineffective leadership cannot be solved with the same *behavior* that created them. The good news is that we can change. Intentional and purposeful self-evaluation is imperative for identifying and correcting leadership lapses and weaknesses in behavior. Correction of those lapses and weaknesses is essential to the success of leaders and their organizations.

Highly effective, influential leaders thrive on daily feedback regarding how others are experiencing them in their leadership behavior. How about you? Are you the kind of leader others want to follow? Would you follow you as a leader? Consistently accepting behavioral feedback may make the difference for you in both your personal and organizational performance. You cannot overcome your performance challenges alone, relying solely on your technical skills.

SKILL BALANCE

There is nothing more destructive to an organization than out-of-touch leaders. You must remain relevant. There is no doubt that our world is changing, and a lot of the change is for the better. We are gaining a new perspective on how we need to behave toward one another in the workplace, with dramatic and positive effects. If you have not yet adapted as a leader, if you are still reveling in off-color jokes or condescending phrases, then you might be in for a rude awakening. Who wants to unknowingly demean or devalue a coworker? Yet behavior lapses demonstrate a failure to adapt and stay relevant during social changes—a weakness that leads to damaged relationships and performance.

Every leader should improve the following three skills (also discussed in chapter 6) in order to develop high-level behavior performance, build effective relationships, and maximize leadership effectiveness.

Dedication to Improvement

Success in every part of life is related to your ability to connect with others. Your success is also directly related to your ability and willingness to learn, change, and grow. Relationships, by their nature, require constant tending. The effort you put into these relationships translates into either a negative or positive experience for other people. When leaders share meaningful learning experiences with their employees, the levels of employee engagement and support for the leader naturally increase.

Undergoing a continuous learning process requires change. Change poses a threat to most people; do not be like most people. Change is always inconvenient and uncomfortable, but being afraid of change is a choice; you cannot learn and grow without being willing to change. New understanding, new knowledge, and new skills can spur constant evolution in the way we think and act. As we noted before, a closed-minded, negative attitude toward continuous improvement can destroy any chance for learning. When there is no learning, there is no growth.

Humility

As we mentioned in chapters 6 and 7, Sullivan and Nomura (2016, 53) wrote powerfully about the connection between humility and leadership influence:

> Only a small percentage of people are continually successful over the long run. These outstanding few recognize that every success comes through the assistance of many other people—and they are continually grateful for this support. Conversely, many people whose success stops at some point are in that position because they have cut themselves off from everyone who has helped them. They view themselves as the sole source of their achievements. As they become more self-centered and isolated, they lose their creativity and ability to succeed.

We believe it is worth asking you again: As a leader, can you give up what you believe is your right to find fault with others and accept personal accountability and responsibility for your stewardship obligation? Can you be open to receiving candid and honest feedback about your own behavior and its effect on those you lead? Can you become excited about letting others help you learn about your own habits to improve the effectiveness of your leadership influence?

Selflessness

Disregard for the welfare and needs of others will prevent you from reaching the highest levels of your performance. Selflessness, putting the needs of others ahead of your own, is essential to creating and sustaining positive and supportive connections with your team. It fuels your performance success.

A PATH TO HIGHER PERFORMANCE

In sum, effective leaders recognize the importance of self-awareness, collaboration, and connection. They spend time focusing their efforts on key areas that strengthen connections with the people they lead to drive performance. They focus these efforts on leadership skills that create behavioral capacity. When you have meaningful relationships with other people, you work more effectively with them. You have a common goal and a consistent purpose. Your efforts are channeled toward a common outcome, and you drive organizational performance to peak levels. This does not mean that technical skills do not matter. It means that behavioral skills (chapter 9) matter more.

KEY TAKEAWAYS

- The inability to interact well with others ultimately can stifle growth and development of people and lead to the creation of hostile work environments.
- In the Toyota Way, the emphasis is on people first.
- Integrated teams working in the conceptual understanding of collective intelligence will improve employee morale and motivation, increase productivity, and improve your organization's safety and quality outcomes.
- Anyone can put together a working group and call it a team, but it takes an influential and effective leader to create and sustain a highly functional integrated team.

- Limited participation by senior leaders in leadership development programs signals a lack of commitment to other team members.

- The real key to improving safety and quality of care and reducing the financial impact of a system fraught with errors is to focus on behavioral skill development under the inspired and focused guidance of effective leaders.

- A key factor of your leadership effectiveness is discovering and developing self-awareness. Leaders need to periodically evaluate their behavior performance in light of their technical performance.

- Change poses a threat to most people; do not be like most people. Change is always inconvenient and uncomfortable, but being afraid of change is a choice; you cannot learn and grow without being willing to change.

PUT IT TO WORK

1. How do you currently evaluate your own behavior and performance? How do you enable others to evaluate your behavior?

2. On a scale of 1 to 5 (1 being "not at all," 3 being "some of the time," and 5 being "regularly"), estimate the level of the following behaviors displayed in your team meetings:
   - Negativity
   - Poor communication
   - Passive-aggressiveness
   - Self-centeredness
   - Lack of acknowledgment

   What emotional reactions do these behaviors create? How do these behaviors affect the relationships among team members?

3. How much time each day do you commit to becoming a more effective leader? What activity do you engage in that is designed to help you get better as a leader? What metrics do you use to ensure you are practicing a variety of new skills that are designed to help you improve your leadership effectiveness?

REFERENCES

Doheny, K. 2021. "Annual Performance Review Bows Out." Society for Human Resources Management. Published January 12. www.shrm.org/resourcesandtools/hr-topics/people-managers/pages/ditching-the-annual-performance-review-.aspx.

Gupta-Sunderji, M. 2018. "It's Time to Get Rid of Annual Performance Reviews." *Globe and Mail*. Published January 29. www.theglobeandmail.com/report-on-business/careers/management/its-time-to-get-rid-of-annual-performance-reviews/article37761480/.

Harter, J. 2020. "4 Factors Driving Record-High Employee Engagement in U.S." Gallup Workplace. Published February 4. www.gallup.com/workplace/284180/factors-driving-record-high-employee-engagement.aspx.

Heifetz, R. A., M. Linsky, and A. Grashow. 2009. *The Practice of Adaptive Leadership: Tools and Tactics for Changing Your Organization and the World*. Boston: Harvard Business Press.

Herbert Walker, D. O., R. J. Reichard, R. E. Riggio, and T. K. Hansbrough. 2020. "Who Might Support a Tyrant? An Exploration of Links Between Adolescent Family Conflict and Endorsement of Tyrannical Implicit Leadership Theories." *Journal of Leadership and Organizational Studies* 27 (4): 340–56.

Myers, C., and M. Doyle. 2020. "Get Adventurous with Your Leadership Training." *Harvard Business Review*. Published February 13. https://hbr.org/2020/02/get-adventurous-with-your-leadership-training.

National Center for Healthcare Leadership. 2019. "Leadership Excellence Networks Overview." https://nchl.memberclicks.net/assets/LENS/2019%20LENS%20Overview.pdf.

Priesemuth, M. 2020. "Time's Up for Toxic Workplaces." *Harvard Business Review*. Published June 19. https://hbr.org/2020/06/times-up-for-toxic-workplaces.

Rowland, D. 2016. "Why Leadership Development Isn't Developing Leaders." *Harvard Business Review*. Published October 14. https://hbr.org/2016/10/why-leadership-development-isnt-developing-leaders.

Sullivan, D., and C. Nomura. 2016. *The Laws of Lifetime Growth: Always Make Your Future Bigger Than Your Past*, 2nd ed. Oakland, CA: Berrett-Koehler Publishers.

Wald, M. 2009. "Report on Pilots Who Overshot Airport." *New York Times*. Published December 16. www.nytimes.com/2009/12/17/us/17pilot.html.

Williams, T. 2018. "Don't Let Low Performers Destroy Your Company." *The Economist*. Updated February 13. https://execed.economist.com/blog/career-hacks/dont-let-low-performers-destroy-your-company.

CHAPTER 9

Behavior Capacity

It's hard to help people who don't think they have a problem. It's impossible to fix people who think someone else is the problem.

—Marshall Goldsmith

OUR PURPOSE, BOTH in writing this book and in our performance and leadership development efforts, is simple: We want to help people achieve a sense of meaning, value, and purpose in their work. That purpose is achieved when we help people create positive and lasting changes in their performance behavior for the benefit of themselves as leaders, the members of their organizations, and the communities their organizations exist to serve. We help leaders improve the quality of their own lives so they can help improve the quality of the lives of others.

At the end of the day, you will never be able to conquer your outside world until you first learn how to calm and conquer your inside world.

Effective leadership behaviors are based on the science of the human brain—how it functions and our ability to control those functions to produce high levels of performance outcomes. We have revealed the cause-and-effect relationships between effective leadership, engagement, and performance. In this chapter, you will discover the key elements of behavior capacity, which is the primary driver of performance.

Behavioral neuroscience is the formal study of how the brain affects behavior. When we understand these effects, we can use that knowledge to drive performance. If you lack the understanding and the ability to manage your fundamental behavior patterns (how your behavior patterns compel you to respond positively or negatively to external stimuli), then you will not gain the benefit of leading with your upper brain.

BEHAVIOR CAPACITY

What if you used your brain to connect with your amazing ability to create and sustain optimal levels of technical skill, talent, intellect, emotional regulation, peace, and joy in your life? You already have the ability to gain control of your thoughts and emotions (Leaf 2013). If you knew how to use this ability, you could change and manage your brain's chemistry and programming, which would result in higher levels of performance behavior.

Behavior capacity is your observable, measurable level of effectiveness in controlling your behavior, both in a work environment and in your personal life. Why place a premium on behavior? For leaders, the operational environment is fraught with complexity, uncertainty, market volatility, and stress. All these factors affect your brain's chemistry and programming (how your brain works). The resulting brain functions affect your behavior response to these factors, and your behavior response affects performance.

Given the challenges in the operational environment, your behavior is the only part of job performance that is completely within your control. Behavior is what you do. Results are what you get done. Using key elements of brain science—focusing on leading with your upper brain—we can create individualized development plans for leaders to consistently achieve effectiveness and sustain high-performing teams. Behavior capacity, then, becomes your strategy to drive performance, increasing the probability that you see the results you desire as a leader.

Science has made huge strides in understanding the human brain and how it functions. For example, we know that the frontal lobes are the centers for rational thinking and self-control. We have discovered that neurotransmitters, or brain chemicals, frame our general state of mind. Our behaviors result from the complex interplay of our genetic makeup, brain chemistry, and brain functions. Just as there is a complex relationship between the brain and behavior, there is also a complex relationship between behavior and performance.

We define *performance behavior* as a measurable connection between the results we desire and the behavior required to produce those results. Achieving the desired results is assured when team members throughout an organization align their work performance with the specific behaviors necessary to perform their work. Performance has two aspects—behavior (the means) and its consequences (the ends).

As Steven Pinker (1997) notes, behavior is the byproduct of thought and mental models. Behavior begins with our internal struggle between competing mental models, which are defined by the way we process external events, including the behavior of others. As we process those models—as we think—we change the physical nature of our brains. By consciously directing our thinking, we can create an internal program that rewires the brain for upper-brain performance—growth, achievement, harmony, development, critical thinking, decision-making, and constructive management of negative stress. In other words, what we perceive defines what we believe, and what we believe guides our behavior. That belief is strongly influenced by what we are thinking, what we know, and the environment at the time.

This relationship between thoughts and behavior explains why individual leader behavior is the single most important predictor of a team's performance. When you mess with the brains of your people in such a way that they must focus on survival, the high-level performance that drives results cannot happen.

Our abilities to think and to choose are powerful forces. Our thoughts—and the behaviors they create—have ramifications that include how our genes are expressed, affecting our immune systems and other physical, mental, and emotional aspects of human performance and wellness.

Behavior capacity, then—which is another way of saying "being behaviorally capable"—is a combination of factors related to how the brain processes thought, perception, and emotion resulting from external stimuli including the behavior of other people. We call the relationship of thought, emotion, and behavior the *cognitive triangle*. Our behaviors, one element of the cognitive triangle, are based on and influenced by several factors: genetic makeup, culture, individual values, and attitudes.

Studies of human behavior reveal four fundamental human behavior patterns (Profiles International 2012, 13). These patterns greatly influence the direction of our efforts, particularly our professional efforts. Since performance is the result of all our efforts, these four behavior patterns explain the variations in how people try to achieve results. A systematic study of these four behavior patterns will explain why upper-brain behavior drives and improves performance and lower-brain behavior blocks performance.

PERFORMANCE BEHAVIOR VERSUS PERSONALITY TRAITS

There have been substantial changes in the workplace since the 1990s. These changes present operational challenges for leaders. For example, the proliferation of virtual teams results in continual variations in the cultural environment. Researchers have had to take these challenges into account while seeking an evidence-based approach to behavior differences that influence leader effectiveness and drive performance.

As we mentioned in the introduction, trait theory—examining the relationship between personality traits and leader effectiveness—is making a comeback. In light of advances in neuroscience that are increasing our understanding of how the brain works, we find the emphasis on a "new and improved" trait theory misguided and lacking scientific merit. Performance and leader effectiveness are directly correlated to behavior, not personality. Behavior, not personality, is what drives performance. That is why your behavior capacity allows you to leverage your technical skills to drive performance.

This is a bold claim, given that human resource and industrial psychology professionals have been committed to personality assessments and trait identification for decades. But in addition to the substantial scientific issues related to associating personality with performance and leader effectiveness, personality assessments have practical issues, as well (Landy and Conte 2015). The most significant has to do with behavior itself—behavior is a function of many different influences (thoughts, emotions, experiences, environment), not just one (personality). Another practical issue is the inability to explain the similarities in outcomes and leader effectiveness between people with different personalities.

Robin Stuart-Kotze (2006) provided a definitive, science-based explanation of the difference between behavior and personality in *Performance: The Secrets of Successful Behaviour.* In the words of Annie Murphy Paul, "there is scant evidence that [personality test] results are useful in determining managerial effectiveness, helping to build teams, providing career counseling, or enhancing insight into self or others" (Stuart-Kotze 2006, 7).

Debating the merits of performance behavior versus personality is not merely an academic exercise. In healthcare specifically, where we lag in patient safety and quality outcomes, real people suffer real harm when performance suffers. If the fundamental premise of personality trait assessments is false, then we have an obligation to alter the practices and models used to measure leader effectiveness and improve performance. We also have an obligation to alter current practices in performance development programs and performance management systems. Despite the claims of those who support personality as the basis of performance, personality assessment results will not help you assess leadership effectiveness, create high-performing teams, provide useful and substantive feedback that helps people grow and develop, or increase the real self-awareness and self-management required for leader effectiveness and job and performance.

Performance behavior is also a necessary element of adaptive leadership. Adaptive leadership is a way of thinking about and engaging in continuous performance improvement, encouraging and helping a team or organization as they make gradual, meaningful changes so they can thrive in challenging environments. Remember what we said about adaptive leadership in chapter 8: The elements of this leadership model enhance the functional capacity of the upper brain. The ability to adapt your leadership behavior to changing environments is the primary factor in creating effective performance. As you climb the ranks of your organization, the requirements of each position are different. Behaviors that made you successful in one job will not necessarily make you successful in your next. Your ability to adapt your behavior to contextual variables and challenging environments is critical to defining your leadership effectiveness and your level of performance.

In this debate between performance behavior and personality, behavior wins in both practical and scientific terms. "Performance behavior means that a measurable connection is made between the result and the behavior that is required to achieve the result" (Webers 2018, 10). When you clearly define the desired result and the behaviors necessary to achieve it, you achieve performance behavior. Think of it in terms of defining a task, establishing the performance standard to achieve the task, and identifying the conditions under which the task is to be performed; when all three are fulfilled, you get the planned result. Performance and behavior are vital to change, adaptive leadership, and achieving improvement and innovation in an ever-changing work environment. By understanding and managing your specific performance behavior pattern, you can connect your performance behavior to key results.

PERFORMANCE BEHAVIOR PATTERNS

We each have a preferred way of engaging with our work, which is expressed through a particular behavior pattern. A behavior pattern is the visible manifestation of a person's significant behavioral indicators and preferred behaviors for performing their job. We can measure these indicators through the specific use of a science-based behavioral assessment, rather than a personality assessment. The value of focusing on performance behavior is that you get to choose your behavior. Every position or job duty incorporates a set of tasks that must be done to ensure success. In general, the completion of these tasks can be enhanced by the effective execution of certain related behaviors. While you do not necessarily choose your personality (who you are), you can choose your behavior (what you do). If you have a behavior that is not aligned with a set of tasks required for producing performance, you can change it.

Leadership is about the behaviors people choose to achieve results. Leadership in action is about getting people to do things differently to continuously improve performance in achieving results. Your leadership effectiveness must be judged by the results produced by your team, and your team members adjust their performance behaviors—either improving or hindering performance—based on what you say and do as a leader. Leadership behavior influences the behaviors—and thus the performance—of others.

Leadership behavior is predictable when you understand the four fundamental behavior patterns. These patterns are differentiated by two key characteristics—behavior focused on tasks and behavior focused on people. Neither of these characteristics is more desirable than the other. Which is more effective depends on the context and operational environment. Ineffective leadership is the result of leaders choosing the wrong behaviors in the wrong contexts.

The most effective leaders are those who can adapt their leadership behavior to changing environments and respond to the legitimate needs of their team members. The alignment of effective leadership behavior with the elements of a value-based culture produces engagement. Engagement, in turn, creates an emotional climate that allows team members to connect and ignite their upper brains for performance (critical reasoning, judgment, creativity, planning, innovative thinking).

Some leaders will be naturally compatible with some employees while requiring slight adaptations to their behavior to bring out the best performance in others. For example, a leader who has a task-focused behavior preference will naturally align with a team member who also has a task-focused behavior preference. Leaders who fail to exhibit adaptive leadership skills may trigger employee behavior that is less than engaged, disconnected from the business and its results, and lacking in effort. The root cause of the employee behavior is the performance behavior clash between the leader and the team member. When this incompatibility is present, both the leader and the team member must adapt their behaviors to increase compatibility and performance results. The research is clear; our performance behavior is significantly affected by whether we view others in a positive and supportive context (upper brain) or as negative or threatening (lower brain) (Cloud 2013).

By virtue of their position, the leader has the responsibility of adapting first. Remember that both leaders and team members have primary behavioral indicators that identify their preferred way of performing their jobs. Knowing these behavior preferences provides a degree of reliability and predictability in how both leaders and team members approach their work and the results they will produce. None of these patterns is more beneficial or more appropriate than another. No one person can exhibit behaviors that are suitable to every situation in changing and challenging environments. Leaders, leading with their upper brains, achieve performance by leading people as they want to be and should be led.

Ultimately, an organization is most effectively led by a team of leaders working in an adaptive and shared leadership model, matching the most effective leadership behaviors and decisions to the most challenging aspects of every situation. The difference between behavior patterns is not "better" or "worse" but rather how each pattern works given the same context. Effective performance in a specific job role results from doing the right behavior at the right time. You cannot alter your personality to match the situation, but you can learn to alter your behavior in changing contexts to maximize your performance effectiveness.

We will now turn to the four behavior patterns and their application to effective leadership and team performance. As a certified user of the Profiles Performance Indicator, we will share how these assessment results map into their four behavior group patterns (Profiles International 2012).

Pattern 1: Assertive and Task Focused

People who display tendencies associated with this behavior pattern are easily recognized by their assertive, direct, and forceful behavior. These people are competitive, self-starters, and action oriented. They are all about getting things done. People using pattern 1 work quickly and are task focused. They also have a power-based mind set; they confront others easily and will not shy away from a great debate opportunity—behavior that can come across as argumentative.

Behavior pattern 1 aligns with defining the objective, staying goal oriented, and producing results. In communicating with others, people using this pattern may struggle with listening to understand. Someone operating in behavior pattern 1 tends to be highly effective at managing processes and less effective at managing the essential elements of interpersonal relationships.

In their upper brains, people using this behavior pattern are very adaptable to changing situations and challenging environments. They will work best with minimal supervision and may struggle to be a fully integrated member of a team. This behavior pattern's key value to a team is the ability to take risks and take initiative. Pattern 1's focus on taking action and bottom-line results will make sure the team gets things done.

In their lower brains, people using this behavior pattern will attempt to dominate conversations, can interrupt others, and may give orders rather than solicit support when working toward a goal. The biggest threat in this mode is being challenged by another pattern 1 leader. Consequently, fear of failure is also prevalent in this behavior pattern. People working in pattern 1 will use the power associated with their position to maintain control of a situation. When working with people using behavior pattern 1, it is important to avoid challenging their control. Offer suggestions in a way that provides them leeway to make their own decisions.

Pattern 2: Assertive and People Focused

People who display tendencies associated with behavior pattern 2 are also easily recognized by their assertive behavior; however, these people are assertive and people focused—genuinely optimistic and enthusiastic. People using this behavior pattern will lead others by inspiring and motivating them.

Behavior pattern 2 works best when people have a great deal of freedom in their work responsibilities. People using pattern 2 will resist being micromanaged and thrive on the social dynamics of work. The pattern 2 upper brain works best when allowed to express high energy, get other people excited about accomplishing a goal, and see everyone enjoy winning as a team. People using this behavior pattern must balance their natural attention to building relationships with maintaining adequate focus on producing results.

In their upper brains, pattern 2 leaders are emotional, creative, approachable, and compassionate, with a genuine regard for the welfare of others. They enjoy the interactions provided by meetings and include their team members' thoughts and ideas. Pattern 2 leaders are generally affable, persuasive, and extremely self-confident. Leaders who use this pattern bring value to a team through a natural affinity for continuous improvement by focusing on change initiatives and influencing others to find better ways of doing things.

In their lower brains, leaders using pattern 2 will hesitate to make difficult, unpopular decisions when under stress. The biggest threat in this mode is rejection, and this behavior pattern may try to avoid that by focusing more on pleasing people than on getting things done. Consequently, the pattern 2 leader struggles to make decisions that have a negative impact on team members and seeks to avoid confrontation and conflict. When working with a leader using pattern 2 behaviors, it is important to ensure they do not lose face in public. They need private coaching and correction to calm their lower-brain fear triggers.

Pattern 3: Cooperative and People Focused

People who display tendencies associated with behavior pattern 3 are easily recognized by their even-tempered, friendly, and team-oriented behavior. Consummate team players, pattern 3 leaders are approachable and people focused. Leaders using this behavior pattern never use their authority to dominate others and tend toward shared leadership. They are constantly looking out for the needs of their team members—sometimes to the point of neglecting their own legitimate needs.

Leaders using behavior pattern 3 prefer predictable and stable work environments, and will struggle with abrupt changes. Unlike rapid-paced and task-focused pattern 1 behaviors, pattern 3 involves a more moderate work pace and a people-focused approach; as a result, these two behavior patterns lack compatibility. People using pattern 3 also tend to avoid confrontation and conflict, which makes it difficult for them to hold people accountable for ineffective work performance. A leader using this behavior pattern often has a high regard for quality and tends to be compliant—a rule follower. They will also display a high degree of humility.

In their upper brains, people using pattern 3 exhibit predictability and patience, and will work best with predictable work schedules. They will be loyal, dependable, agreeable, and effective listeners. They will avoid interpersonal aggression, preferring to accommodate the needs of others. People using pattern 3 will think things through before responding and are rarely impulsive, even under stress. A pattern 3 leader brings value to the team through their highly developed listening skills and by creating close, highly developed, long-term relationships.

In their lower brains, people using pattern 3 will oppose change and seek to maintain the status quo. They will resist impulsive decisions that they believe will disrupt known practices and established performance standards. Their desire for safety and security makes it difficult for them to take prudent risks they fear might threaten the welfare of their team members. When working with people using behavior pattern 3, it is helpful to coax them out of their comfort zone and pursue realistic stretch goals. Their biggest fear is sudden and disruptive change. These people need direct, objective, and candid feedback that is focused on their performance, not their person, as they often take feedback personally, but the humility that characterizes this behavior pattern makes them coachable and teachable.

Pattern 4: Analytical and Task Focused

People who display tendencies associated with behavior pattern 4 are easily recognized by their task-focused behavior and their drive for precision, accuracy, and perfection. People using pattern 4 have a high regard for rules, regulations, guidelines, and protocols. They are extremely conscientious and are strict about timeliness and rule following. Pattern 4 leaders are firm in their beliefs about right and wrong and will not compromise their core values. They value relationships built on trust and integrity. You get to be dishonest with someone using behavior pattern 4 once. If you are deceitful with them a second time, they will deny you any effective connection or relationship with them.

People using this behavior pattern often ask many questions in meetings—usually, very detailed questions focused on the specific topic and objective of the meeting. They do little socializing and can conflict with pattern 2 people, viewing the social needs of pattern 2 as a waste of time. Pattern 4's overall demeanor is careful and reserved, and people in this pattern tend to make decisions slowly and only after weighing all the facts and alternatives.

In their upper brains, people using pattern 4 have an eye for detail and approach their work in a systematic, organized, and logical way. They are excellent problems solvers and view most work objectives as puzzles to solve. Pattern 4 uses facts and logical arguments to overcome objections. People in pattern 4 think before responding and need time to process information because they check facts, weigh pros and cons, and look for trade-offs in every situation. They maintain their composure and rarely overreact. They bring value to the team through their attention to detail and their moral compass.

In their lower brains, people in pattern 4 are overly sensitive to any criticism of their work. Their biggest fear is not being perfect, which makes it difficult for them to receive coaching feedback on their performance. They will display perfectionistic tendencies and struggle to admit when they are wrong and have made a mistake. Their drive for consistency will make it a challenge for them to try something new. Someone in pattern 4 and their lower brain will rarely change a process or accept a new idea without substantial data to support the rationale for change. Under prolonged stress, this behavior pattern becomes withdrawn and distant, disrupting team members' ability to maintain sustained efforts toward outcomes. In this state, a pattern 4 leader will overthink and over-analyze a problem, delaying the decision-making process, and fear taking decisive action.

PERFORMANCE BEHAVIOR TEAMS

The performance behaviors described in the four behavior groups have tremendous impact on the outcomes that teams produce. A high-performing team has a strong sense of balance, drawing on the preferences of a diverse group of individuals who are joined together by a common purpose and direction. Creating teams with a balance of the four behavior patterns should be part of diversity and inclusion initiatives. A team's ability to work effectively is greatly influenced by the compatibility of the individual behavior characteristics of the team members. Two critical factors affecting a high-performing team are team cohesion and team productivity. While a team can adjust to accommodate compatibility issues, the fewer adjustments necessary, the more effectively the team will function.

In managing a team, the more behavior data leaders have about the characteristics of the team members, the more focused the management of that team will be. One of the primary causes of a lack of team unity and productivity is an overabundance of one or more of the four behavior patterns.

When no one on a team, including the leader, exhibits behavior pattern 1, the team may struggle to connect with its purpose. Team members will have difficulty adapting to change and managing stress. They will lack clarity about the direction and scope of their work, will be slow to execute, and will struggle with productivity. They may fail to better themselves through training and development opportunities and become stagnant and unfamiliar with technological trends that improve job performance.

When a team has no access to pattern 2 behavior characteristics, they may struggle to develop trusting relationships with each other and may create artificial barriers that preclude open and honest disclosure and feedback. The "all work, no play" demeanors dominating this team may create poor work–life balance and result in an unhealthy, stressful work environment. Instead of expecting the best and preparing for the worst, they expect the worst and are surprised when anything good happens. Sometimes, expecting negative outcomes becomes a self-fulfilling prophecy.

Without pattern 3 behaviors, team members may place too much emphasis on the project to the detriment of the people. These unbalanced teams tend to place too much pressure on team members to perform. Lacking patience and composure, team members become cynical and overly cautious, resistant to change, inflexible, and closed-minded. They may fail to effectively problem solve because safe and nonthreatening environments are lacking, stifling communication. The resulting levels of negative stress may also result in errors, missed deadlines, underperformance, and reduced productivity.

When pattern 4 behavior characteristics are missing from the team, people may make mistakes due to oversights in compiling, reviewing, evaluating, or applying information. The team can place too much emphasis on a finished product without consideration for careful analysis and study. This team will resist continuous performance improvement activities and struggle to replicate desired results consistently. Finally, this team will disregard a deliberate planning process, rushing to complete projects without regard for safety and quality.

THE KEY TO ORGANIZATIONAL PERFORMANCE

In all four patterns, the expression of behavior—upper brain or lower brain—is directly related to the neuroanatomy of the brain and how it creates performance neurochemical cocktails. Various neurotransmitters and neuropeptides contribute to how we form relationships, meaning they play a major role in creating high-performing teams. The key neurochemicals contributing to upper-brain performance behavior are endorphins, dopamine, serotonin, and oxytocin. The primary neurochemical activating lower-brain impediments is cortisol (Lambert 2018).

Endorphins serve as an analgesic, relieving physical pain. They have played a major role in human survival and the perpetuation of the species. They allow us to be risk takers, to overcome physical obstacles. Endorphins also help us form the social attachments that are essential for creating high-performing teams.

Dopamine is sometimes called a chemical messenger. Our nervous systems use dopamine to transmit messages to nerve cells. Dopamine plays a role in how we feel pleasure. We receive a dose of dopamine when we eat food; that is why eating can be a pleasurable activity. It also explains why dining with other people—mixing endorphins and dopamine—is a pleasurable social event. In terms of performance behavior, dopamine allows us to be goal oriented. Every time you check off something on your task list, you get a little dose of dopamine. Dopamine also plays a major role when an organization pursues a lofty, aspirational vision. Endorphins and dopamine both play a major role in the task-focused elements of our lives and work.

Serotonin and its neurochemical twin oxytocin support the people-focused elements of our lives and work, giving us our relationship rhythms. Serotonin plays a key role in mood regulation—promoting feelings of well-being, joy, and happiness. Serotonin helps us create trust, leading to the bonds of friendship and the foundation of a high-performing team. Serotonin provides us empathy and compassion in relationships.

Oxytocin is also related to empathy, trust, and relationship building, as well as helping to regulate our sleep patterns and boost our immune system. Researchers often call oxytocin "the love hormone." Oxytocin motivates us to perform acts of kindness, generosity, and benevolence. Every time you perform, receive, or witness an act of kindness, you get a dose of oxytocin. Research on oxytocin is far from complete. Preliminary studies suggest that oxytocin plays a dual role in managing responses to circumstances in times of low and high negative stress (Uvnäs-Moberg and Petersson 2005). During times of low stress, oxytocin physiologically rewards those who maintain good social bonds with feelings of well-being. During times of high social stress or pain, it may lead people to seek alternative, more effective social contacts. Just as endorphins and dopamine are responsible for instant gratification and can explain the fight response to stress, serotonin and oxytocin are responsible for creating lasting feelings of calm and safety, helping to explain the flight response to stress.

Researchers call both serotonin and oxytocin the "social neurochemicals." Mix a neurochemical cocktail without them, and you achieve success in the absence of meaning, value, and purpose. Toxic leadership behavior will inhibit the release of serotonin and oxytocin in team members, damaging the team's culture. Studies show that low levels of serotonin result in disengagement, burnout, and depression. As a leader, when you mess with the brains of your people, you do so at your own performance peril.

Finally, we want to discuss cortisol and its influence on the disruptive elements of the lower brain. Cortisol is a naturally occurring steroid hormone that plays a key role in the body's stress response. Best known as the "stress hormone," cortisol plays a major role in mediating blood pressure, glucose metabolism, immune response, and much more. Our immune systems are neurologically sensitive to stress that is generated by fear, loss, doubt, and other elements of toxic thinking. Toxic thoughts and emotions interfere with the body's natural healing processes.

Toxic stress also puts undo pressure on the heart. Not only a pump, the heart also has at least 40,000 nerve cells and produces its own neurochemical—atrial natriuretic factor (ANF), an atrial peptide. ANF is a "balance hormone" that regulates many of the brain's functions and triggers behavior. When threatened by something in your environment, your body instantly begins preparing you to respond to the threat. The limbic system, namely the amygdala, functions as a processing center that signals a range of responses, including the release of hormones such as adrenaline and cortisol.

Cortisol is important for your body to function normally, but too much cortisol can be bad for your health and impede performance behaviors. The outcome of chronic fear and its related stress is chronic doses of cortisol. Cortisol is not supposed to linger in our bodies. When a person lives in perpetual fear, loss, and doubt (which a toxic boss and toxic work environment can stimulate), the effects of cortisol on the heart, immune system, and the digestive system can cause lasting physical harm. Whereas oxytocin boosts our immune system, cortisol compromises it. Whereas dopamine lights up the upper brain for performance, cortisol literally turns off the upper brain. This poses a serious threat to the well-being of people working in dysfunctional organizations. It also poses a serious threat to any organization's performance, but can have particularly dire consequences for healthcare organizations in terms of failure to deliver safe, high-quality patient care. The constant flow of cortisol to the human brain is bad for people and bad for performance.

FINAL NOTE

Performance requires more than your skill, talent, and intellect; it requires you to have a highly developed sense of behavior smarts so you can function as an effective leader. Leaders have two fundamental daily requirements—managing the process context (technical skills) and the people context (behavior skills). The behavior skill set is a combination of a leader's ability to manage thoughts, emotions, and behavior. A leader's inability to manage the people context through highly developed behavior skills affects their ability to manage and execute process context (technical skills) to produce results.

Behavior performance as outlined throughout this book takes an integrated and systematic approach to linking effective leadership with engagement to drive performance. As you discovered in part I and part II, behavior capacity is a matter of how the brain functions, in terms of both the wiring and the neurochemicals that result in either upper-brain or lower-brain behaviors. Performance behavior, growth, and development derive from the prefrontal cortex managing neurochemical cocktails of endorphins, dopamine, serotonin, and oxytocin. The limbic system, primarily through the amygdala, governs threat response, fear, and stress.

The upper brain is built for performance, displaying analytical and technical ability. The upper brain also grasps concepts quickly, creates vision, and manages complexity. The lower brain responds to survival needs and threat responses. It shifts our focus away from the technical and analytical elements of the upper brain, instead focusing us on surviving when survival is paramount. These are not trivial distinctions. Effective leadership results from a cause-and-effect relationship between performance behaviors in the upper brain (growth and performance) and blocking behaviors that reside in the lower brain (fear and survival). Management of the tension between these two competing operating systems provides the spark to energize, engage, and enhance performance throughout the organization.

Every leader knows there is a better, more effective leader within, waiting to grow and choose development-expressing behaviors that will create higher levels of engagement and performance in their teams. An effective approach to discovering the better leader within you is the use of an executive coach. The environment in a coaching engagement makes it safe for you to explore the key aspects of your personal and professional aspirations, talking about the things that matter most to you, your team, and your organization. Effective coaching can have several valuable benefits: improved self-awareness, self-regulation, and social skills; increased motivation and empathy; clearer thinking; and more effective leadership behaviors.

A universal truth in the life cycle of high-performance organizations is that individual breakthroughs drive organizational breakthroughs. Reducing the variability of leadership performance is critical to aligning your strategy with key performance objectives and with the performance results you desire as a leader. Effective leadership behavior is the means to a greater end, particularly in healthcare: safe practices, high-quality care measures, and patient care experiences that create high levels of service satisfaction.

You can get everything else right regarding the technical skill elements of performance—recruiting and retaining the most talented team members, having the most innovative strategy and the most robust financial margins—but if you lack effective leadership behavior, you will never obtain the high level of performance you are technically capable of achieving. Highly effective leaders exhibit behaviors that create highly effective relationships. They cultivate an organizational culture that allows those relationships to thrive and drive organizational engagement. They use the power of engagement as leverage to create organizational behavior capacity. By flexing and accommodating the four fundamental behavior patterns, effective leaders learn how to lead the upper brains of their team members to higher levels of performance.

Effective leaders are always on an improvement journey, looking to discover the better leader within. We are on that journey, too. Will you join us?

KEY TAKEAWAYS

- We want to help people achieve a sense of meaning, value, and purpose in their work.
- At the end of the day, you will never be able to conquer your outside world until you first learn how to calm and conquer your inside world.

- When you mess with the brains of your people in such a way that they must focus on survival, the high-level performance that drives results cannot happen.
- Behavior, not personality, is what drives performance. That is why your behavior capacity allows you to leverage your technical skills to drive performance.
- Behaviors that made you successful in one job will not necessarily make you successful in your next.
- As a leader, when you mess with the brains of your people, you do so at your own performance peril.
- In managing a team, the more behavior data leaders have about the characteristics of the team members, the more focused the management of that team will be.

PUT IT TO WORK

1. In 1948, Bertram Forer conducted a study with his students, seeking to validate the accuracy of personality testing. The results, published in the *Journal of Abnormal Psychology* the next year, demonstrated what is now called the *Barnum effect,* or sometimes the *Forer effect,* in which people give high accuracy ratings to vague, generalized personality descriptions when they are told those descriptions are personalized to them (Forer 1949). Read the original paper (https://doi.org/10.1037/h0059240) or the discussion in the online Encyclopedia Britannica (www.britannica.com/science/Barnum-Effect) to understand why behavior, not personality, is the key driver for performance.

2. Describe your team's communication approach. How does it help or hinder the dissemination of information? What tools and resources are available to your team to facilitate

communication among members and between members and other cooperative partners?

3. Are you aware of the performance behavior patterns of your team members? How do these patterns complement or conflict with each other? What effects do these differing patterns have on your team's unity, cohesion, and productivity?

REFERENCES

Cloud, H. 2013. *Boundaries for Leaders: Results, Relationships, and Being Ridiculously in Charge.* New York: HarperCollins.

Forer, B. R. 1949. "The Fallacy of Personal Validation: A Classroom Demonstration of Gullibility." *Journal of Abnormal and Social Psychology* 44 (1): 118–23.

Lambert, K. 2018. *Biological Psychology.* New York: Oxford University Press.

Landy, F. J., and J. M. Conte. 2015. *Work in the 21st Century: An Introduction to Industrial and Organizational Psychology*, 5th ed. Hoboken, NJ: Wiley.

Leaf, C. 2013. *Switch On Your Brain: The Key to Peak Happiness, Thinking, and Health.* Grand Rapids, MI: Baker Books.

Pinker, S. 1997. *How the Mind Works.* New York: W. W. Norton & Company.

Profiles International. 2012. *Profiles Performance Indicator and Team Analysis Applications Manual.* Waco, TX: Profiles International.

Stuart-Kotze, R. 2006. *Performance: The Secrets of Successful Behaviour.* London: Pearson Education Limited.

Uvnäs-Moberg, K., and M. Petersson. 2005. "Oxytocin, ein Vermittler von Antistress, Wohlbefinden, sozialer Interaktion, Wachstum und Heilung (Oxytocin, a Mediator of Anti-Stress, Well-Being, Social Interaction, Growth and Healing)." *Zeitschrift für Psychosomatische Medizin und Psychotherapie* 51 (1): 57–80.

Webers, N. C. W. 2018. *Performance Behavior: The Lean Methodology for Continuously Improving Performance Behavior*, 2nd ed. Netherlands: Foras Media.

Index

Note: Italicized page locators refer to exhibits.

neurochemical bartenders, 114–15, 183; performance capacity and, 147; team engagement and behavior of, 115. *See also* Ineffective leaders; Leaders

Effective leaders, making of, 156–62; collaboration and, 161–62; contingency theories of leadership and, 158–59; leadership styles and, 159–61

Effective leadership, 5, 8; craving for, 143; culture of purpose and performance excellence and, 149; in engagement equation, *18,* 109, 114; five fundamental myths of, dispelling, 157; individual leader behavior and challenge of, 50, 147, 155, 183, 192, 223–24; performance and, 182; performance behaviors and, 148; primary function of, 88, 102; three fundamental processes of, 157. *See also* Ineffective leadership; Influential leadership; Leadership; Leadership effectiveness

Effective leadership behaviors, 192; cause-and-effect nature of, 28; personal well-being, performance outcomes and, 111; to practice daily with team members, 193

Effective leadership development: integrated and comprehensive methodology for, 41, 42

Effective leadership equation, *18, 28,* 41–50, 181; behavior and, 50; effectiveness and, 46–47; leadership and, 48–49; performance and, 43–45; self-awareness in, *18,* 28, 31, 42, 85; self-management in, *18,* 28, 31, 42, 85

Effective managers: ineffective leaders *vs.,* 35–39

Effectiveness: assessing, three proactive questions for, 46; effective leadership equation and, 46–47

Egocentric leaders, 64

Einstein, Albert, 214

Electronic health records: implementation challenges and, 175

E-mail management: focused attention and, 99–100

Emotional intelligence: leadership success and, 13

Emotional intelligence movement: initiation of, 42

Emotional pressure, 145

Emotional regulation: limbic system and, 70

Emotional resonance: prioritizing, 13

Emotions, 28, 53, 225; becoming aware of, 61; behavior as byproduct of, 182; in cognitive triangle, 66, 67, *67,* 224; managing, behavioral skill set and, 4; managing, self-awareness and, 64; negative, 76; nonconscious mind and, 71; positive, 76; regulating, 69, 70, 75–77, 84; taking ownership of self and, 94; toxic, 237

Empathy, 47, 68, 77, 120, 193

Empedocles, 14

Employee engagement, 109, 111–12, 146–47, 205; average engagement score, 108; compassion, respect, and, 190; defining, 116–17; effective leaders and, 127; employee satisfaction *vs.,* 107–8, 112, 116; leadership effectiveness and, 108; servant leaders and, 167; superior results and, 114, 128; in United States, 19; what it is not, understanding, 116. *See also* Engagement

Employee engagement, creating, 117–25; compassion and, 120–21; fulfilling fundamental human needs and, 117, 125; hope and, 122–25, 128; security and stability and, 121–22; trust and, 118–19, 128

"Employee Job Satisfaction and Engagement" report (Society for Human Resource Management), 108

Employees: putting first, 176

Employee satisfaction: description of, 107–8; employee engagement *vs.,* 107–8, 112, 116

Empowerment: employee engagement and, 116; team, evaluating, 152

Endorphins, 236, 237

Engaged employees. *See* Employee engagement

Personal development plan, 7, 222–23
Personality: behavior *vs.*, 160, 182;
    as poor indicator/predictor of
    performance, 160, 171
Personality assessments: practical issues
    with, 225
Personality Change Consortium, 160
Personality testing, 160
Personality traits: performance behavior
    vs., 224–27
Personal purpose statement, 23, 84;
    crafting, 91–92, 104; inner self-
    management and, 89, 91–94
Personal self-management: as your inner
    game, 88
Perspective: reframing and refocusing,
    105
Pinker, Steven, 223
Playfulness, 145
Policies and procedures: desirable
    employee behaviors and, 45
Poor customer (patient) experiences:
    disengagement and, 125
Positive emotional triggers: behaviors of
    effective leaders and, 114
Positive emotions, 76
Positive psychology, 73, 122
Positive thoughts, 74
Posterior cingulate cortex: distractions
    and, 100
Potential: upper brain functions and, 145
Power: compassion and, 189–90
Power of Neuroplasticity (Helmstetter),
    192
Practice of Adaptive Leadership (Heifitz,
    Linsky, and Grashow), 209
Predictability: loss of, 52
Prefrontal cortex, 29, 183, 185, 239; focus
    and, 100; igniting, self-awareness
    and, 64. *See also* Upper brain
Primal Leadership (Goleman), 13
Primary care providers: risk of suicide
    and, 126
Problem-solving performance factor: key
    improvement suggestions for CEO
    and, 37; performance and, 43
Process capacity, 183; leadership
    development programs and, 196;
    managing relationship between

behavior capacity and, 177, 179;
    undeniable link between behavior
    capacity and, 182, 198
Process-oriented leaders, 64
Productivity: decreased, disengagement
    and, 125
Productivity performance factor: key
    improvement suggestions for CEO
    and, 37; performance and, 43
Professional development plan, 200
Profiles Performance Indicator, 229
Project Oxygen, 42
Promises: keeping, 148, 193
Psychological safety: engagement and,
    19; promoting, 17
Psychosomatic death, 75–76
Purdy, Amy, 92
Purpose, 191; achieving sense of, 221,
    240; constancy of, 149; effective
    leaders and, 148; growth and, 165;
    high-performing teams and, 168;
    hope and, 123; impact of culture on
    engagement and, 135; upper brain
    and, 145. *See also* Meaning
Purpose-driven culture: developing, 188,
    197, 199

Quality of care: behavioral skill
    development and, 197–98, 218;
    shift in Joint Commission's survey
    process and, 11–12
Quality performance factor: key
    improvement suggestions for CEO
    and, 37; performance and, 43

Rage, 75
Reappraisal (or reframing): emotional
    regulation and, 76–77
Recruitment, 139, 178
Reengineering projects: failures of, 136
Relational self-management: as your
    outer game, 88
Relationship building, 5
Resilience, 124; training, 126; undermining,
    hopelessness and, 123
Resistance: change initiatives and, 51
Respect, 108, 193
Responsibility: personal, inner self-
    management and, 94

About the Authors

Michael E. Frisina, PhD, has authored more than 50 papers and published articles on leadership and organizational effectiveness. He is a contributing author to the Borden Institute's highly acclaimed textbook series on military medicine. He is a visiting scholar at the Hastings Center in New York, a visiting fellow in medical humanities at the Medical College of Pennsylvania, a John C. Maxwell Top 100 Transformational Leader for 2018 and 2019, and a two-time educational grant awardee of the American College of Healthcare Executives. Dr. Frisina serves as chairman of the Health Administration Advisory Council for the American Military University. He is also an executive in residence with the

University of North Texas School of Public Health. You can contact Michael at michael.frisina@gmail.com.

Robert W. Frisina, MA, is a principal in the Frisina Group and executive director at the Center for Influential Leadership, with primary responsibility for program development and research in leadership effectiveness and organizational development. He is a member of the US Army Reserve and served as a civil affairs specialist with the Second Brigade Combat Team in the 101st Airborne Division in southern Afghanistan. Robert is a graduate of Clemson University, Norwich University, and the John F. Kennedy Special Warfare Center and School. Prior to his current position, Robert served as a legislative and policy adviser to the governor of South Carolina. Robert can be contacted at bfrisina@gmail.com.